"The perils of finding one's way home—the Cyclops and Sirens we encounter, the self-doubt—have long been one of the primary themes of the world's great literature. The 14 riveting stories in *COMING HOME* provide valuable insight for the modern traveler on how to succeed in that journey back to our true home in God, and the need for a trusted Companion who can show us the way." –Andrew Papageorge, Founder, *GoInnovate!*

"*COMING HOME* invites you on an intimate journey and welcomes you to a sacred place that is story and soul, transcendence and truth. Each conversation shines a light on the questions we ask about our own meaning and purpose, our own hopes and fears in voices that are you, that are me. Blessing and inspiration, this gem of a book inspires, transforms, and offers countless opportunities for insight and personal growth." –Mark Leary, Sculptor, Storyteller, www.MarkLearyDesigns

"*COMING HOME* has at its heart the divine moment when a true devotee of God finds in Paramahansa Yogananda the One who loves them unconditionally and will help them fulfill their Divine potential. Each tale is unique, full of heart, humility and humor, and candor. Every soul who's walked this path will be moved to tears of gratitude as they remember how they, too, have been chosen and are loved. Full of timeless spiritual treasures, this book is meant to be read again and again." –Shelly Girard, CPM, MPH , LM Certified Professional Midwife

"*COMING HOME* is a testament to Paramahansa Yogananda's living presence and how his universal yoga teachings provide support and strength to those that keep him near and dear to their hearts. These sweet, intimate stories will bring great solace and inspiration to spiritual aspirants enthralled by the ancient wisdom of Yoga and its capacity to transform anyone's life. Books like this help us see the Divine hand behind life's many challenging events and keep us living a Godward life."
–Mas Vidal (Maheshananda) Teacher, Ayurvedic Practitioner, Author, *Sun, Moon & Earth: The Sacred Relationship of Yoga & Ayurveda* www.dancingshiva.com

"With the first words in *COMING HOME*, I got 'God bumps' that stayed with me throughout the book. These poignant stories take you from suffering to hope, from fear to love; the questions raised, the miracles revealed go beyond dogma and prejudice. They keep you on the edge of your seat and take you deep inside yourself to divine answers only God can give."
–Bethany Grace, www.Joyfulviolinist.com

"Reading *COMING HOME* was an experience of effortless peace—something akin to gliding across the water in a rowboat at dawn, a ride that took me to a state of contentment and satisfaction. What else could I ask for from a book?" –Dr. Scott Walker, DC, Founder, N.E.T.

"*COMING HOME* is a book I've always believed needed to be written. Margaret has curated an intuitive collection of the joy and peace and depth that living your life with Paramahansa Yogananda brings to so many. The stories not only inform and inspire, they make you more aware of how the Guru is truly guiding you every day in subtle ways that make you smile and sometimes make you laugh." –Marianne Gottlieb, Teacher

Coming Home

Finding Shelter in the Love and Wisdom
of Paramahansa Yogananda

To Sarah
With Love
Margaret

Coming Home

Finding Shelter in the Love and Wisdom
of Paramahansa Yogananda

MARGARET WOLFF

. White Pearl Press .

Encinitas, California

First Edition

ISBN: 978-1-7355083-0-6 (paperback)
ISBN: 978-1-7355083-1-3 (ebook)
Library of Congress Control Number: 2020914570

Coming Home is published by:
White Pearl Press, Encinitas, CA
www.ComingHomeStories.com

For information about bulk sales and permissions, please direct emails to: Margaret@ComingHomeStories.com.

Cover artwork: "East End," painting by Donna Young, www.donnayoung.com

Cover design, layout and typography: Teri Rider & Associates

Permission to use the photograph of Paramahansa Yogananda in Pittsburgh in 1926 is granted by Self-Realization Fellowship, 3880 San Rafael Avenue, Los Angeles, CA 90065-3219, U.S.A.

DEDICATION

For the waiting, thirsty ones.

"What greater satisfaction could one have, than when the heart is aflame with yearning for the unknown God and He actually comes as guru? What greater consolation could one receive, than to find when one's devotion is strong and incessant the Inconceivable Infinite manifests in the visible form of guru?"

—Paramahansa Yogananda
The Second Coming of Christ

CONTENTS

Paramahansa Yogananda
(January 5, 1983–March 7, 1952)
Pittsburgh, 1926

Photo Courtesy of Self-Realization Fellowship

About Paramahansa Yogananda

Paramahansa Yogananda was born Mukunda Lal
Ghosh on January 5, 1893, in Gorakhpur, India. His
fervent longing for God drew him, at seventeen, to Swami
Sri Yukteswar Giri, the enlightened master who guided his
spiritual journey. Eight years later, Mukunda took vows as a
monk of the ancient Swami Order and was given the name
Yogananda—bliss, *ananda*, through divine union, *yoga*. The
religious title *Paramahansa* was later bestowed on him by
his guru.

In 1920, Yogananda set sail for America to serve as
India's delegate to an international congress of religious lead-
ers in Boston. His maiden speech was so well received he
began crisscrossing North America, then the globe, bringing
India's ancient meditation techniques for attaining a personal
relationship with God to thousands of spiritual seekers of
every religion who—then as now—were searching for a universal spirit of love and understanding amidst troubled times.

In 1925, Yogananda established Self-Realization Fellowship (SRF) in Los Angeles, California, the non-profit, non-sectarian spiritual organization that disseminates his teachings throughout the world. Except for a brief return to India in 1935 - 36, he spent the remainder of his life in the United States teaching, writing, and compiling a home-study course known as the Self-Realization Fellowship Lessons. Yogananda's *Autobiography of a Yogi*, the compelling story that details his personal search for God and the divine potential that exists within every human being, was named one of the 100 Best Spiritual Books of the Twentieth Century. In 2014, the award-winning documentary on his life and work, *Awake: The Life of Yogananda*, was released worldwide.

Paramahansa Yogananda is widely regarded as one of the preeminent spiritual figures of our time. Though he passed away on March 7, 1952, monks and nuns of the Self-Realization Fellowship Order continue to conduct lectures, classes, and retreats on his teachings and provide spiritual counsel to SRF's thousands of worldwide members, students, and friends.

To learn more about Paramahansa Yogananda and the work of Self-Realization Fellowship, please visit http://www.yogananda.org.

Songs of Kabir XXVII II. 81

It is the mercy of my true Guru that has made me to know the unknown;

I have learned from Him how to walk without feet, to see without eyes, to hear without ears, to drink without mouth, to fly without wings;

I have brought my love and my meditation into the land where there is no sun and moon, nor day and night.

Without eating, I have tasted of the sweetness of nectar; and without water, I have quenched my thirst. Where there is the response of delight, there is the fullness of joy. Before whom can that joy be uttered?

Kabir says: "The Guru is great beyond words, and great is the good fortune of the disciple."

—Translation by Rabindranath Tagore

Prologue

In the summer of 1995, 4,000 attendees at the annual Self-Realization Fellowship World Convocation listen with rapt attention as Brother Anandamoy, one of Paramahansa Yogananda's direct disciples, tells a story about a man named Andy Anderson's first encounter with the great guru. The year is 1949. Andy is supervising a handful of young monks—including Brother Anandamoy—building Self-Realization Fellowship's Hollywood Temple when Paramahansaji arrives at the construction site. The men gather around the Master. He tells them a few stories, one after the other, nothing about religion, then takes his leave so they can continue their work.

Andy is deeply moved by the stories, clearly astounded by what he heard. He takes Brother Anandamoy aside and discreetly asks him if he understood what the Master was talking about. Brother tells Andy they were "nice stories," and Andy realizes Brother does not know why he asked him the question. Andy is embarrassed. He laughs then explains, "Why, that man just told us the whole story of my life, including all the mistakes I made! He knows *everything* about me!"

Brother looks at Andy and laughs. Now he understands. He tells Andy he had a similar experience during his first interview with the Master.

"He told you stories?" Andy asks.

Brother tells Andy that during the interview, the Master asked him many questions about his life and his studies. But given the way the questions were phrased Brother realized that Paramahansaji didn't need any additional information because he already knew everything there was to know about him.

Brother waits for the laughter in the lecture hall to subside, then moves to the heart of his story. He tells Andy there was more to his conversation with the Master that was as astonishing to him as realizing Paramahansaji's omniscience: Though he knew everything there was to know about Brother, the Master had no judgment about what he knew. There was only understanding—and love.

This is Andy's experience of the Master as well. He pauses for a moment to think about what Brother has told him, then says, "You know, I want to become a member."

Brother's voice is very measured now as he speaks to the audience, as he tells us what went through his mind those many years ago. He had witnessed the moment every disciple of Paramahansa Yogananda holds in their heart; the moment they are "handpicked" by the guru. "And I thought," says Brother, "There it is! *That's* why Master came!"

The audience sits unmoving as Brother picks up the pace. He tells us that Great Ones like Paramahansa Yogananda were once just like us, once subject to all the temptations of the world we still face. As a result, they have utter sympathy for our "human follies." They have love and understanding—even humor—for our entanglements. They also know that discrimination and self-control, that meditation and spiritual effort, lead us into the waiting arms of Spirit. And, the example of their lives proves to us that we, too, can secure our freedom in God.

Brother presses forward; he draws a parallel between Andy's experience and the story in the Bible of Phillip's response to meeting Jesus for the first time. "Follow me," said Jesus. And Phillip does. Andy chose, as Phillip did, to follow his guru because he, too, had gotten the call.

Brother gives us a moment to let this analogy sink in. It's a moment of profound tenderness. Most everyone in the room knows what it feels like to "get the call." Like Andy, one day out of the blue something extraordinary happens in our lives that proves, beyond any shadow, beyond any doubt, that everything about us is known by an avatar of all-seeing proportion, and that *our* avatar is a living, loving presence beyond anything, beyond anyone we could imagine. We, too, feel "handpicked." Discovering Paramahansa Yogananda, discovering his teachings, is for each of us like coming home.

In a true disciple, there is no sense of self-importance or superiority at being "handpicked." In fact, it's quite the opposite. By the time you become familiar with Paramahansa Yogananda, you are mindful of the dissatisfaction and impermanence inherent in external experience. You may be wanting, confused, even disillusioned, adrift or mired by a sense of disconnection and loss. When you discover your true connection to Paramahansaji, you are astounded, as Andy was astounded, that someone knows everything about you—and loves you anyway. The details of your origin story—the birth of your discipleship—are so up close and personal, so intimate and tender, that when it happens to you, you are "beguiled by an infinite ingenuity" and convinced of Yogananda's omniscience and unconditional love. There is no other way to explain what's happened to you. You have been seen. You have been found. Life suddenly makes sense. You are chosen not because you are exceptional, or even because you are in need, but because you are loved. And you know, as the Indian mystic and poet Kabir says, "The guru is great beyond words. And great is the good fortune of the disciple."

No matter where our search for happiness takes us, no matter who or what we call our path, we all yearn to know three things: that we are part of Something Greater, that we are cherished, and that our lives have been and can continue to be—come what may—meaningful. With this in mind, I began writing *Coming Home.*

As of this writing, I have been a disciple of Paramahansa Yogananda for forty-four years. I've heard many origin stories in my time, listened gratefully to the revelation of details that prove Yogananda's living presence in the lives of his devotees, that almost always leads to the moment when the storyteller looks at me—often with tears in their eyes—and says, "it was like coming home."

Many origin stories involve reading *Autobiography of a Yogi*, Yogananda's own story of coming to his guru, Swami Sri Yukteswar, and the training he received under his tutelage. As a writer and as a therapist, I believe in the magic and the power of a story well told—its ability to inform, yes, but also its ability to transform a heart in unexpected ways. Reading Paramahansa Yogananda's story and keeping company with him in your heart puts you within reach of his spiritual magnetism, his wisdom, and his compassion. You feel heard. You feel safe. You belong. You open your heart to "undreamed of possibilities." It really *is* like coming home.

The narratives in this book are not just stories, they are actual experiences of Divine Grace. They urge us to "build our house upon a rock," to say "Yes!" to our soul again and again and again, to bear witness by how we live our lives. It's a privilege for me to make this journey—to be a pilgrim who walks in Paramahansa Yogananda's footsteps and a privilege to tell these stories in his name.

"The characteristic features of Indian culture have long been a search for ultimate verities and the concomitant disciple-guru relationship."

—Paramahansa Yogananda
Autobiography of a Yogi

ONE

A Powerful Thirst

I was born in Nairobi, Kenya, in East Africa circa forty years ago. My great-great-grandparents moved to Kenya from Gujarat in the north central part of India in the late 1800s. They made the long, arduous journey by ship, ended up in Zanzibar—an island off the African Coast—and began importing spices from India into Africa.

In those days, spices were like gold, and my great-great-grandparents built a lucrative family business. At some point during the 1950s one of the ships sank. There was no insurance to cover such things, and the business went bankrupt. My dad had to drop out of school to support the family. He moved to Mombasa in Kenya to work in the hotel industry and was introduced to my mom. Theirs was an arranged marriage; Mom was given a choice between three suitors and she chose him because he was the most handsome.

Over the years Kenya became very politically unstable and my parents wanted my younger sister and I to have a good education and professional opportunities that wouldn't be available to us in Kenya. When I was eleven, we moved to Vancouver, British Columbia to be with my extended family. This is where I grew up.

English was my first language. I spoke Swahili in Kenya, but we spoke Kutchi at home—the Indian dialect of my ancestral homeland. I was born an Ismaili Muslim, a sub-sect of Shia Islam. It is a monotheistic religion: one God, Allah; one prophet, Mohammed—the Messenger of God. We follow the lineage of Prophet Mohammed down to his present descendant, the Aga Khan IV. We speak of him as the *Imam*—the religious and spiritual authority, a guide, rather than a guru—who disseminates the values and practices appropriate for the time we live in that can help us balance the inner life with the outer life, the spiritual with the material.

Our faith-based practices are the key elements to creating the material stability that provides the space and time to further our spiritual efforts and serve humanity. So, from the time I was a child, my family regularly went to the mosque for prayer, meditation, and spiritual service. We also have special prayers throughout the month: New Moon has special prayers, the week after New Moon has special prayers, and so on. When we lived in Kenya, I also went to the mosque almost every evening with an elderly neighbor because I loved being there and I loved being in the presence of God.

When we moved to Vancouver, I went to the mosque almost every day with my grandma. After prayers, she would socialize with her friends and I'd volunteer to do some simple job at the mosque like washing dishes—whatever needed to be done—because I could focus my mind on repeating the name of God. I'd get into a zone where it was just God and me, and I loved it.

This routine continued throughout my university years. High school and college were pretty crazy, and I felt safe and comforted at the mosque. It's also where I felt a sense of belonging. I didn't know how to acclimate to Western society when we moved to Canada; I didn't understand things like dating or sleepovers or going to the movies. My parents held on tightly to their version of what "a good girl" did. Their mantra was, "We can't have our daughter out gallivanting!" Going to the mosque also gave me the freedom to come and go as I pleased.

I went to college in Vancouver and became an accountant. I had no interest in getting married. I wanted to be my own person, build my career, and focus on my spiritual growth. I went back to school while I was working and got my CPA, got promoted at work, and moved to the head office. I loved to travel and really enjoyed seeing how God's creativity manifested in the world. I started socializing more with friends from work. It was a full and busy life. I could no longer go to the mosque every day with my grandma, but my faith practice remained steady.

Eventually I got engaged, but it ended after a short time because the relationship wasn't spiritually oriented. Though I'd achieved all the material goals that are a benchmark of success, I had a great thirst for something more. I began asking myself what life was all about and delved deeper into my spiritual quest. I explored various forms of meditation and did a lot of spiritual reading. One Christmas, a friend got a copy of *Autobiography of a Yogi* at a gift exchange we attended and I asked her if I could read it. I read it cover to cover in two days and loved it! Everything Master said resonated with me, but I had no idea there was more to his teachings than the *Autobiography*—an organization, the Lessons, temples, and so on—so I continued searching.

Fast-forward three years to 2015. By this time, my entire family was heavily into setting me up with a potential suitor. I kept telling them I wasn't interested in anyone unless he could be a spiritual partner, but no one understood what I meant by this. I was very content with my life and work, and was not going to settle on someone just because he had a good job or went to the mosque!

Around that same time, several of my cousins got married. Indian weddings go on for months. I knew I'd have to go to a profusion of events and every auntie in my family would be trying to set me up with some guy. So I got the idea to join an online spiritual dating service so I could easily and truthfully say to my aunties, "I went on a couple of coffee dates with a guy, so I'm fine. Don't set me up." It seemed like a great plan.

As it turned out, that's how I met my husband, and that's how I came to the path. Our first coffee meet-up lasted six hours. Most of our conversation was about our spiritual practice. He told me right away he belonged to SRF, and the way he talked about Master's values, principles, ethics, and focus on meditation was so aligned with my own thinking I was floored! I thought, Wow! This is the real deal! And he *does* all this! And he's a *real* person!

SRF also gave me the vocabulary to talk about the spiritual life in a way I'd never been able to do before, and talking with someone who could express all the things I'd been thinking about showed me that what I'd been thirsting for actually existed. A lightbulb went on! I began going to SRF services and meditating with him. As our relationship deepened, so did my understanding of SRF.

In the beginning, I went through a period of questioning. What I was hearing in the services and from my future husband resonated deeply within me. The teachings were so completely true they were never a question for me. But I wondered if practicing another teaching meant I was being disloyal to the faith I was born into. I finally realized that when I stay in the Divine Presence and take the name of God—whether that's Allah or the Heavenly Father—I'm being loyal to my True Self, my greater Self, a Self not limited by form. I was building on what I already believed, and learning to do that in a deeper way. Practicing Master's teachings was, thus, not a rejection of anything I loved, but an expansion of what I already knew and loved. Once I understood this, I felt SRF is where I'm meant to be.

As I continue to practice the teachings, I discover the answer to any questions I might have about the path is always, on a conscious level, that SRF is Universal Truth. On a superconscious level, the answer is always the experience of the teachings that comes in meditation. And now that I understand what's happening in meditation, I can go deeper into the experience.

Master's teachings make the spiritual life a partnership. I'm learning to communicate and participate and belong to something that resonates deeply within me. It's more intimate. I've talked to God since I was a child, but now I have a relationship with God, the closeness to the Divine I always yearned for. That intimacy is my a-ha! This is it! This is home!

Being on the path and being an Ismaili Muslim are not mutually exclusive. I participate to the fullest in both. It's up to me to balance these different elements. I still do my prayers and practice the values and ethics of the faith. Now, on the path, I have even more I can do that helps me draw closer to God: I have the Lessons, the Temple, the *satsangs*, the kirtans, and—most special of all—I have the gift of taking Kriya! Life is rich and full.

My husband came up with a story about Master and the Aga Khan IV walking on the beach in Encinitas that captures it all for me: Master says to the Aga Khan IV, "I have this guy for one of your spiritual daughters," and the

Aga Khan IV says, "I think this is going to work." They were in cahoots! It's like the Aga Khan IV was metaphorically telling me, "Okay! You're ready now to meet Master, and he'll get you where you need to be."

Meeting my husband was not a chance encounter. I was set on a spiritual partner; I just never realized it could manifest in such a true way. God wanted this to happen and I'm not going to mess it up!

My favorite quote from *Autobiography of a Yogi* says it all for me: "God is Love. His plan for creation can be rooted only in love. Does not that simple thought rather than erudite reasonings, offer solace to the human heart? Every saint who has penetrated to the core of Reality has testified that a divine universal plan exists and that it is beautiful and full of joy."

It can be a little scary to see how much power you have within you, what you can do in partnership with God—when it's God's will. I already understood on a surface level that everything is God's will, but when I coupled my commitment to His will with my firm intention and highest desire, I experienced how powerful we all really are. Once I understood that, I understood I had a responsibility to use my power to do the best I can, to fully satisfy my thirst for God because the world needs seekers of God. Then the rest is God's will. *InshaAllah*: it is the will of God—the joyful, beautiful will of God.

TWO

Practice Makes Perfect

I'm a local. I was born in 1952 in San Diego County, forty-eight days after Master left the body, and have lived in Cardiff and Encinitas my entire life. I have three children and four grandchildren. My husband passed away six years ago. I was a Montessori teacher for fifteen years before my kids were born.

All four of my great-grandparents were homesteaders in Encinitas. My great-grandmother got an insurance settlement in 1880 after she lost her husband in an accident in a meat-processing factory in Chicago. When she remarried, her new husband convinced her to go to California—to the "Promised Land." They hopped a train and ended up in Olivenhain, a rural community on the east end of Encinitas. They had five children, including my grandmother Amelia. Grandma got two hundred acres of farmland as a wedding present and had three sons, including my father.

My grandfather's parents came from Luxemburg and had a ranch along Quail Gardens Road. They ran the Stagecoach Stop and my grandfather was the sheriff. During prohibition he had a still and sold moonshine at the beach. That's how Moonlight Beach got its name—or so the story goes. Their coming here was all part of the cosmic set-up that paved the way for me to come to Master.

My family life was unhappy and I often fended for myself. I spent a lot of time with Grandma Amelia. She was a very ethical woman and a great comfort to me. She taught me to cook, to grow things, and to care for the land. Master was all around me as a child, though I didn't know it then. Grandma had a friend, a famous photographer who was also the brother of actor Jim Backus. Her husband died before I was born, so Mr. Backus was like my substitute grandfather. His mother donated and played the organ in the SRF Golden Lotus Temple until it fell into the sea in 1942, so he must have been there, too. We'd drive down the Coast Highway past the SRF Café and he'd point at the lotus towers and say, "That's a really nice place. You remember that!"

My great-aunt Camilla knew Master and went to the Golden Lotus Temple on Sundays. She was the town schoolteacher. Her little daughter was killed on the train tracks in 1939 and Aunt Camilla saw the whole thing. Master reached out to her in his divine way and helped her through the tragedy.

When I was in ninth grade, my speech teacher gave my class an assignment to give a three-minute talk about someone we admired. I'd seen Master's picture in the newspaper so I walked to the SRF Meditation Gardens and got a brochure about him. I looked at his picture and said, "Gee, he's as wonderful as Jesus" so I gave my speech about him. I got a B.

When I was in the Gardens, I remembered I'd been in the Hermitage six years before. There was a girl in my third grade class who lived with her parents at the Golden World Colony—that's what they called Master's place then. That year she invited our whole class to the Colony for her birthday party. We played games with the nuns in what's now Swami's Park, then we toured the Hermitage.

When we walked into the living room, I was very surprised because Master's house looked just like my house, only bigger—the same walls and beamed ceiling, the same fireplace, a rose garden, a koi pond, a big dombeya tree, and a flagstone path around the outside of the building. The architect who built the Hermitage also built several smaller homes in the neighborhood, but I had no way of knowing that then. When we went into Master's bedroom I stood at the foot of his bed and rubbed my hand along his bedspread. Two boys from my class started jumping on Master's bed! I stood there thinking, Oh, that looks like fun, but I was too shy to do anything. The nun hosting us heard the ruckus and shooed the boys off the bed.

My family was Lutheran. I went to Sunday school and we said a little prayer at dinner, but that was the extent of my religious education. When I was twelve we got a new pastor who told us God made the world in seven days and the earth was 7,000 years old. I raised my hand and asked, "But what about the dinosaur bones?" He lost his peace right there and kicked me out of Catechism! I walked home and told my parents what happened and the next thing I knew my grandmother arranged for a new pastor.

By the time I was fifteen, I was longing for something to believe in. It was the days of Joni Mitchell and Bob Dylan. My parents didn't care what I did, so I started going to love-ins and concerts and smoking pot, hitchhiking up and down the Coast with girlfriends. The music became my inspiration and support.

One day I met a guy who actually paid attention to me. One thing led to another and on the eve of my sixteenth birthday I got pregnant. Two months later I realized what happened and told my mom. She told my dad. They were furious and insisted I give up the baby. By this time, it was clear the baby's father was unstable. I had no one to turn to. Once I began to show I dropped out of high school.

The birth was difficult. I was in the hospital two weeks. I wanted my son to have a good life, a better life than I could provide on my own. It was very painful, but I gave him up for adoption. I knew it was the best thing for him.

I returned to school and tried to move on with my life, but I was very depressed. One day I went for a walk on Pipe's Beach with a girlfriend. A boy she knew walked over to us and started talking to her. He looked at me and said, "Here's a great book. Can I give it to you? I think you'll like it." He gave me the *Autobiography*, then walked away with my friend.

I sat down on a rock, opened the book, and started reading. It was like I was starving and was suddenly eating the best meal of my life, a ten-course gourmet feast! I read the first ten chapters, stood up, looked over at the Hermitage above me on the cliff, and all of a sudden I realized whose book I was reading! I said, "Oh my God! *He* wrote that book! Up *there*! Wow!" Finally, I had something I could grab on to, a direction for my life. I walked home, ate my supper, and finished reading the book.

Even though I didn't understand what a guru was, I knew intuitively Master was like Jesus and that I needed to follow him. Once I started putting two and two together, I saw that Master had been part of my life even before I had a life. At first, I felt I wasn't worthy of him, that I was "damaged goods." In 1969, having a child out of wedlock was a shameful thing. Changing that view of myself has been a big part of my journey. I *am* deserving! And I know whatever mistakes I made, whatever bad things happened, Master has always loved me. I was then, as now, a work in progress.

I sent for the SRF Lessons right away. Because I was under eighteen, my mom had to give her OK. Practicing the techniques helped me a lot; they raised my vibration. But I had no idea what spiritual *sadhana* entailed. I have dyslexia. I was in high school trying to catch up and it was hard to read everything. I had no one to share the path with and no support for my journey. Though I was living in the spiritual haven of SRF, I got lost in the false charms of the world and fell off the path.

In 1972, I started going to Thursday night service again. In those days, services were in the Retreat Chapel. Brother Anandamoy was the minister. Brother Premamoy, Mukti Ma, Brother Bhaktananda, Sister Shanti, even Sri Daya Mata gave services. Brother Anandamoy and Brother Premamoy were such noble men. Being around them helped me realize how I wanted to live. They had what I wanted. So I started reading my Lessons and practicing the teachings.

I met my husband the day I took Kriya. He was smitten right away, but I was scared to get married. Then one day a little lightning bolt struck me with regards to him. We got married eight months later.

Once our kids were born, I stopped teaching and my spiritual practice centered on raising them and caring for my husband who had health problems. I knew Master was with me. I meditated and served at the Temple when I could, but I couldn't read the Lessons or go to services regularly for years. When my husband died I called out for Divine aid and was rescued. I had a spiritual experience that changed my perception of myself and what I was to do with my life. I was coming home to Master a second time.

It's an inner life now. I attend every service and meditation at the Temple. I study the teachings and serve Master's work. The path is my life, my love, my everything. I'm closer to Master than I ever was.

My relationship with Master makes for a very busy life. It's a variety show. Some days I nag him. Some days I'm his little kid. Some days we're gardeners. Some days are a science project—there's a lesson I need to figure out or a glitch in my personality I need to identify and release. I love it when I have an a-ha moment, but I surrender to Divine timing. Meditation has become my favorite thing in the world. I'd rather do that than spend two weeks in Hawaii!

I may never know all the pieces of the puzzle and I still cry about things, but I understand now that there's a bigger picture going on I don't always see in the moment. Sometimes, when I least expect it, my prayers are answered. After almost fifty years of wondering about the son I gave up for adoption, Master brought him back into my life. Unbeknownst to me, he began looking for me the day I had that spiritual experience that awakened my soul. Like a pebble making a ripple in a pond, my heart's desire to know my son rippled through creation and created a wave of love that brought him to me.

I've read Master's autobiography often over the years, and it continues to inspire me. It's like home to me, a loving home I've taken refuge in since I first read it in high school. I especially love reading the words of the gurus. Sometimes, I memorize something they said and use it as an affirmation. Repeating their words over and over in this way puts me in touch with their living presence. New perceptions happen from time to time as I do this. It's "Ever new," as Master says. And practice makes perfect. I'm grateful for it all.

THREE

Love One Another as I Have Loved You

I am forty-four years old, originally from Portland, Oregon. I moved to L.A. when I was twenty-one. I am, by profession, a marriage and family therapist.

I'm technically an only child, but I have an older half-brother and sister, siblings from my mother's previous marriage, who visited us often when I was a kid. We're close like siblings are. When my parents divorced, my mother married a man with four older children who also became like siblings to me. At times, the seven of us all lived together; at times, I lived as an only child.

Both my parents were teachers. My father eventually went into child protective services; my mother remained a teacher until she retired. They met in grad school, drawn to each other because they were both deeply motivated by social change and service to the world. These values inspired me as a child and later influenced my choice of career.

My father was raised Baptist. After serving in Vietnam, he became interested in Eastern philosophy and began seeking a teaching, a way of life that would bring him peace. He read the *Autobiography* in graduate school and by the time I was born, he'd contacted Mother Center and started the SRF Portland Center in our home with a few other local devotees. My mother grew up Catholic. Compassion and kindness motivated everything she did—then and now. She was not overly religious, but she was comfortable enough with her practice to attend church. Neither of my parents wanted the other to adopt a practice they weren't drawn to, so they agreed to each follow their own path and let me decide what worked for me. I had no restrictions from either of my parents about what I believed, something I really appreciated when I was growing up.

I was very interested in religious things as a child. Because the SRF group and Sunday school met in our home, I was surrounded by Master's books and photographs from the beginning of my life and the teachings became the foundation of my spiritual understanding. Because SRF is so broad, I was open and curious about all religions. I went to church with my mother on Sundays and the rest of the week my home was, so to speak, my Temple.

About the time I was five, I began to notice that my friends and their families were involved with spiritual practices different than my own, and I began dipping into what they were doing. When I was in other religious spaces, I paid close attention to how people interacted with their scripture, their reverend, and their fellow fellows, and looked for that same feeling of love and connection in them that I had with Master. What they were doing seemed fun to me and I enjoyed the reverence people had for their God, but I really liked the silence of meditation. Being silent with other people felt powerful to me, and I wanted the opportunity to meditate with others, so when I was twelve, I began attending SRF adult services.

I've been in SRF all my life. I've heard many stories about how other devotees connected with God and Guru, particularly at some point in their lives when they needed something to believe in. When I tried to pinpoint when that connection occurred for me, I realized I'd felt connected to Master for as long as I can remember. Once I could read—or at least listen to recordings of Master and the monastics—everything I read or heard spoke to what I already believed—namely that universal, omnipresent, unconditional love was the essence of everything and everyone. My child's mind enjoyed that what I believed was so well represented in Master's teachings, and I was comforted that what I believed was happening in my home. This inner resonance is why SRF stuck with me no matter what other religions I came in contact with.

I realize, now, this was a somewhat unconventional way for a young kid to think about their relationship to the path, but it made sense to me. Though I was born into a life that allowed me early access to Master's teachings, I was also born into a life that was very conflicted. My parents are from different races and married at a time in history when being together wasn't socially acceptable. Their marriage was most definitely not accepted by their families, and they were both disowned when I was born. Though my parents were very loving towards me, I felt the hatred others had towards us as a family and felt regret and responsibility for my parents' struggle. Having Master constantly in my home and in my heart reminded me that what people said about us simply wasn't true. Because of my relationship with Master, I could feel there was something beyond others' hatred: something bigger, something that mattered more than the opinion others had of us. My pain was always met with the awareness of Master's presence. He was right there for me.

In this way, my story is like the stories I've heard about Master showing up when a devotee needs him most. I needed to feel his love right from the beginning of my life, and he made sure I would. The world wasn't doing me any favors in terms of my identity, but I spent very little time questioning who I *really* am because there's always been Master who saw me, who saw who I am.

As long as I can remember, the opportunity to sit with what I felt when I expanded beyond myself in meditation was something I wanted to do. I also liked being reflective and introspective. I had my own altar with photos I loved— *The Last Smile, God's Boatman*, Master with the little dog in his pocket. My spiritual practice got more serious when I started coming to California for the boys Summer Youth Program and I got the meditation techniques. This gave me more to do while I was meditating and I enjoyed that. Being around a bunch of kids who were having the same experience I was also meant a lot to me and was formative in terms of my wanting that kind of fellowship in the future.

My father was usually my Sunday school teacher and the conversation we had in class often continued during the week. His regular practice was so appealing to me, like a comforting blanket wrapped around me. I noticed the positive effect meditation had on him and the commitment all the adults who came to our house had to practicing the techniques. There has never been a time in my life when I didn't think meditation was this nice, warm, wonderful, loving space to be in.

Starting when I was about ten, my mother and I began having deep conversations about religion and spirituality, about Christianity, about Jesus and other saints and sages. She wanted to know what I understood about God and what I thought about what she understood. Our conversations inspired her to start coming to services and take the SRF Lessons. Now she's an SRF member, but she still has the saints she's loved all her life.

Though others were spiritual examples for me, Master was really the source of my spiritual interest. My father felt Master should guide me, not him. Everything I did spiritually was my choice versus something I was told to do or did with my parents. I had my personal, independent spiritual life, and they had theirs because it's for each of us to form our own relationship with God.

I kept my spirituality secret from my school friends. I had one friend in high school that was Buddhist and a vegetarian, but she was the only person my age in Portland who knew what I was doing. Sometimes it was lonely, but I came to understand that most people in the world are struggling with what it means to have a relationship with God, especially in a material world where everybody worries about money and relationships and identity. Master's teachings are very high and deep. Though I was committed to this life for myself, I never wanted anyone to feel I was judging them, and I didn't want any judgment coming my way.

I often thought about becoming a monastic, but I had a strong desire that began in childhood for a career in space exploration that ran parallel to my spiritual life. I was attracted to monastic life and to every monastic I came to know, and I was definitely attracted to Master and the life he lived, but I felt called to pursue a career in space. When things didn't work out, the possibility of a monastic life really opened up for me. I did a lot of introspection and counseling with the monks to figure out what I should do. In the end, I felt there was something outside the ashram, some work in the community that was right for me. I also had a desire to be married and have a family. I don't know if that's in store for me, but I knew I couldn't fulfill that desire as a monastic.

Eventually, my path became clear and I returned to school and pursued a career in psychology. Now, I do workshops on the power of empathy and self-care, and help people deal with the implicit bias and complex trauma that is a consequence of societal and cultural oppression. I talk about race and class and privilege—things that played a big role in my own life—and I emphasize the self-acceptance and understanding a contemplative process can provide when life is difficult.

Master's teachings helped me know and accept who I really am and to develop empathy for people who were acting hurtful towards me—to understand their limitations and express forgiveness and love. I want to help others learn to experience the benefits a level of pause and introspection can bring into one's life. We still have to face our challenges, but a healthy sense of self gives us something to bounce our challenges off of. I feel sure this is a good path for me because when I go to work, I expand my own self-understanding and I feel a comfort similar to what I felt as a child when I began meditating.

I began reading the *Autobiography* when I was very young. To learn about the life of someone I felt so close to was extremely touching to me. The story of Master meeting his master, Sri Yukteswar, has always been a great inspiration to me. Sri Yukteswar tells Master he will love him unconditionally and asks Master if he will return that same love to him. Master makes that promise. Then Sri Yukteswar asks Master to promise to take his head on his lap if he ever sees him slipping. Their interaction perfectly describes that the guru-disciple relationship—that unconditional commitment—goes both ways. I appreciate how vulnerable Sri Yukteswar was in asking Master to help him.

It's really special to open your heart to God's unconditional love, but it's more special to give your heart to God. It's not an easy thing to do. The world can be frustrating sometimes. There are times I'd rather leave it all behind. Then I think about what Sri Yukteswar asked of Master, and I understand that part of being unconditional is to trust Master and give him my heart in those difficult moments. That trust is part of the promise I made to him and to God, and it's then that God and Master and the world need my heart the most.

FOUR

His Promise

I was born in the summer of 1926, so I'm 93 years old. I trained as a medical technologist and that's what I did until I retired in 1991. I took twelve years off, though, when my children were young to care for them.

I grew up in Saint Paul, Minnesota, the middle child of three kids. My father was a milliner during the 1930s, at a time when ladies still wore hats. He had stores in small towns all around Minnesota and a few stores in the Dakotas. He made a good living. Even though it was the Depression, he was able to sell hats for two or three dollars each because women would not go to church without a hat.

My mother stayed at home with the kids when we were young, then helped my father at his store after we got older. When hats went out of fashion and he closed his business, my mother went to business school then went to work for a doctor.

My father's father was a Lutheran minister, so we were definitely Lutheran. Our church was at the end of our block and we walked there every Sunday. I learned a lot about Jesus at church, of course, and I attended confirmation classes, but we never talked about God at home. I got the idea for what I should do and not do from my mother and from the Ten Commandments, but I didn't think much about what I heard in church once I got home.

My father was an alcoholic, but we didn't realize it when we were growing up. No one talked about those kinds of things back then and we didn't know what to do about his behavior. He had quite a temper and I was often afraid.

I had two husbands: the first one for twenty-seven years, then we divorced; the second one for eleven years, then he died. I have five children and two grandsons.

My first husband was Catholic. We got married when I was twenty-two. He insisted right away I join the Catholic Church. My parents didn't put up much of an objection; so I took some lessons from a priest, found them to be acceptable, and joined up for nearly twenty years. My husband, children, and I all went to church together every Sunday because we were told that if we didn't we would be committing a mortal sin. The priests were pretty crabby and not very nice to us. I eventually got tired of all that and stopped going to church. My husband stopped going too; it was never anything really deep for him—or for me.

By the time I was in my late forties, I began to really miss being in a church. I looked around for some place else to go and joined the Christian Reformed Church. One day I realized they believed that the only people who were going to go to Heaven were the people who were Christian Reformed. I was so surprised they thought that! It was too rigid for me so I left. I joined the Unity Church and went there on my own for about fifteen years until I came to Master.

After I'd been married for a few years I realized I'd made a bad choice with my first husband. He was an alcoholic like my father. I asked him to stop drinking but he refused. Things kept getting worse as time went by. I thought I was supposed to stay married to him because that's what my mother did. Years later, after I came to Master, I read something he said about how people often go headlong into a wrong marriage for the wrong reasons, and I realized that was exactly what I'd done. I was young when I met my husband and didn't know what I was doing, and I was in a hurry to get out of my parents' house. There I was, forty-nine years old, afraid to leave him and afraid to be alone. Fortunately, I met some people who helped me feel better about myself and, in time, I gathered the courage to get a divorce.

A few years later, I married my second husband. He was a very nice man and we had a trusting friendship for eleven years before he passed away. I thought about getting married again and dated a little bit but after a few years of that, I said, "That's it! I'm going to buy a dog and pay attention to God."

A few months later, I became acquainted with Yogananda. I'd started going to a hatha yoga class through the adult education program in my community. Then I went to a yoga conference and learned about meditation. I started going to a meditation center in Minneapolis near where I lived. I liked meditation a lot, but the center had been involved in a big scandal and I wanted to be with good people, so I stopped going there. One day I went to a woman's house for a study group and when I walked into her living room I saw *Autobiography of a Yogi* on her coffee table. When I picked up the book I immediately had the feeling this was something I should pursue. I bought the book right away and started reading it but stories about miracles weren't for me so I stopped reading. Not that miracles are a bad thing! It's just that what I was after was love, not miracles.

A few months later, I saw a flyer on a bulletin board at the community center about a talk on how to spiritualize your life. That sounded good to me so I showed up for the lecture. But instead of talking about that topic, the speaker showed the movie, *Glimpses of a Life Divine* about Yogananda. I really liked that movie and decided SRF was my path, so I signed up for the SRF Lessons. About a month later the Lessons started coming to my house. As soon as I began reading them something clicked. I immediately knew Yogananda was my guru. And that was that. It was 1998. I was seventy-two years old and I'd finally found my path back to God.

I stopped going to all the other groups and classes I was attending and studied the Lessons at home on my own. At some point, I went back to the *Autobiography* again and finished reading it. When I read what Master said about Kriya Yoga I thought, I'm going to take this initiation at the first opportunity I can get. So I did. In 2000, I went to Chicago when SRF had a monastic tour there and got Kriya from Brother Anilananda. I started going to the group here in Minneapolis about six months later. There I was, my whole life looking for love in all the wrong places, and I found it in God.

I think everybody realizes they need love, but how and where we get it is hard to figure out. My parents' love was pretty conditional. Their expectations were very high and I only got love if I was obedient or good. My first husband was definitely not a loving partner. My second husband passed away earlier than I expected. Kriya was the best, most loving experience of my life. It felt so wonderful. I felt so happy. I'm not self-realized yet, but I keep at it. Master helps me out a lot.

Once I started going to the group, I got very involved. I became coordinator when I was eighty-two. I needed some experienced help to get the job done because I had no idea how to organize anything or how to even run a meeting. Someone in the group who was very experienced in organizational work stepped up to help me. We had a big public event in 2010 and the monks came to our Minneapolis Center. Planning all that was challenging, but together we pulled it off. It turned out to be fun. I learned to smile more. I liked being coordinator because I felt I was doing his will every day.

Some people say I'm bossy, but I let Master call the shots because he's always right. He tells me what to do and say. He talks about how your tongue can do a lot of damage, so I love knowing what we are not supposed to talk about. If I have a problem with someone, I examine my part in the disagreement—how I contributed to it. I don't blame. I detach. I ask Master to remove any hurt, and he does. I'm also calmer. I don't get depressed like I used to. If I do, I just ask Master to help me get rid of whatever sad feelings I have.

I live in a place now with a lot of people my own age. I have a few friends. I have my stretching routine. I watch baseball in the summer. But there's a limit to what a ninety-three-year old can do. I'm happy to be by myself, to not be married. I can pursue my meditation without anybody asking me what I'm doing. I spend quite a bit of time reading about Master's teachings and meditating. I think about Master a lot and thank him for being with me. I know what happiness is now and how to be happy. I'm committed. And I'm very determined. Most people don't realize where their happiness lies. I'm so glad I found him and he told me what's what!

My favorite story from the *Autobiography* is the one about Kashi. Master told Kashi not to leave the school at Ranchi because he knew something bad would happen to him if he left. He asked Master to promise to find him if he died, and Yogananda finally said okay to that. Then, sure enough, Kashi's father pressured him into leaving the school, and he got Asiatic cholera and died. When Master heard what happened, he used this special yogic technique and found Kashi even though his soul was now living in a new body inside a new mother's womb.

I think this is a great story about how the guru promises to find his disciples life after life, about his love and loyalty for all his disciples—not just for Kashi. I'm ninety-three. I've only been on the path twenty-one years. Since I've not become self-realized yet, I figure I'll probably have to do it in my next lifetime. I've talked to Master about coming to me in my next life when I'm younger so I can have more years to practice his teachings, and that I'd like to start off being born in an SRF family. I also called Mother Center one day to talk about some things that were on my mind, and they told me he would meet me when I die. That sure is great to know.

The first time I read Master's poem, "God's Boatman," in his poetry book, *Songs of the Soul*, I was just floored. He promises he will come for us even if "… one stray brother is left behind"—and sister, of course. I thought, who of us can say we love like that? I sure can't!

I don't doubt Master will do that for me. I know he will find me. I trust him completely. He says if you cry for God day and night, you can be liberated in a short time. We don't have to be perfect. We just have to be sincere. And do our part. That's what I want for my next life.

FIVE

Child of Eternal Lightening

I was born in Jamestown, New York, sixty-nine years ago. I've been married forty-two of those years to my life partner. We have two children and another child who ascended, and four grandchildren. I'm a registered nurse, board certified in holistic medicine. I've been an SRF devotee for forty-eight years.

My mother's father was the family patriarch. He had a very successful furniture business and our family was prominent within the community. He arranged my parents' marriage. I was the eldest of their two children.

After my grandfather died, we moved to Seattle. I was six. It was a difficult move and I began taking riding lessons to help me cope. I rode and showed horses all over the country until I was eighteen. It never occurred to me I'd have any other kind of life than with my horses. I had everything I ever wanted except for my dad's drinking.

My parents fought a lot about this. Then, when I was twelve, my grandmother and her new husband came for a visit and whisked my father out of our home and out of my life. I was never allowed to say his name in my mother's presence again.

After that, everything I'd loved about my life was in shambles. My mother sold our home. My riding ring was gone. We returned to Jamestown and my mother married the man who was her first suitor. I dearly loved her new husband, but my dad was my best friend. I missed him terribly. A few months after returning to Jamestown, I called and asked him if I could live with him. He sent me a plane ticket and off I went. I didn't tell my mother what I was doing. My father was blamed for my leaving and my mom and I were estranged for many years.

My dad's drinking grew worse and he became progressively more debilitated. I couldn't watch it happening so I, once again, immersed myself in riding. I'd graduated high school by then and was taking random college courses thinking I might find something else to do with my life besides riding. Sitting behind me in a consumer law class was this guy I thought must be the most beautiful person in the whole entire world. Over time, we became good friends. One day, he told me he'd been drafted and was thinking about going to Canada. It was 1970 and his was a common response to the draft. He went in as a conscientious objector, trained as a medic, and was stationed in Germany, but witnessing the casualties aired in from Vietnam was more than he could bear. He went home on leave and told his family he was going to Canada. I packed up my little Volkswagen, crossed the border, and met him in Vancouver.

We eventually connected with the Doukhobors, a group of Russian immigrants who grew their own food, built their own houses, home-schooled their children, and lived close to God. I didn't know much about God then. I'd read *Siddhartha*, *The Yoga Sutras of Patanjali*, and *The I-Ching*, but that was it. My mother was Presbyterian, my dad was Episcopalian, but God was not part of their lives. Their "religion" was being appropriate—appropriately educated, appropriately dressed, appropriate relationships—and financial respectability. I knew there was something beyond that, something more meaningful, but I had no clue what that was.

By 1972, I was married with one child and another on the way. We had a cabin, a garden, a well, and knew how to eat out of the woods. My husband worked as a medic on the Arctic Pipeline and was gone three months at a time. Every once in a while I'd drive twenty-five miles into town and get provisions. One day, I walked into a funky little bookstore in town and noticed a pile of books stacked on a rickety table. *Autobiography of a Yogi* was on the top of the pile. I picked it up, thumbed through it, put it back on the table, then stood looking at it for the longest time. It cost $3.65, too much money for a family that lived on $90 a year! Maybe some day, I thought, but not today, then got in the truck and drove off. A mile down the road I thought, I cannot live without that book, so I went back and bought it. I had no idea why.

I drove home, put my son to bed, started a fire, and settled in with the book. As soon as I started reading it I thought, Oh my God! I *knew* there was more to the story! This is who we are! Why we're here! What life is about! I couldn't wait to turn every next page. I read and slept, read and slept until I finished the book. Then I thought, What am I going to do *now*?

I noticed Mother Center's phone number in the back of the book, drove to the nearest pay phone, dropped my quarters in the phone and dialed the number. A little voice said, "Self-Realization Fellowship, may I help you?" I thought I was going to faint.

I said, "Are you really real?" And the voice said, "Yes dear, we are."

I said, "I just finished *Autobiography of a Yogi*. What am I supposed to do next?"

"Well dear," she said calmly, "we have some Lessons you can take." I thought, Lessons, yes! She said, "What's your address?"

We had a rural PO box in the boonies of British Columbia and I'd never gotten mail there, but I gave her that address and my Lessons started coming. They became everything to me.

When my husband came home several weeks later, there was a strange disconnect between us. Something had changed. I showed him the Lessons, he was mildly interested, but he wasn't the starry-eyed devotee I'd become. Shortly thereafter, we moved to an SRF community on Vancouver Island. I was in heaven, but my husband grew more distant. His time in the service haunted him. Ultimately, he decided to be on his own and asked what I wanted to do. All I could think of was, I want to go to Encinitas. He put us on a bus with enough money for a month's lodging in a motel a mile from the SRF Retreat in Encinitas.

The morning after we arrived, we took a cab to the Retreat and walked into the office. Sister Shanti greeted us. I told her my story, she made a phone call to some local devotees, and we ended up living with them for about six months. I went to meditations, to convocation and got my Kriya, and listened to Master's chants—always asking Master what he wanted me to do next. One day, it became clear I was supposed to return to Jamestown. I was resistant, at first, but then I thought, I asked Master to guide me, and now he's told me what to do and I'm telling him no? I can't tell him no. So, I called my mother and stepfather and they sent us money for bus tickets back to Jamestown. Shortly thereafter I decided to enroll in nursing school.

But this isn't the end of this story. Master had something else up his sleeve! An old friend of my stepbrother's called to say, "I hear you're back in town." How I'd lived and what had occurred in my life was unheard of in Jamestown circles, but he wanted to get together. He was kind, tolerant, non-judgmental, always interested in listening, very thoughtful, very smart, and wonderful with my children.

My spiritual path didn't shock him. I knew his whole life. We were delivered by the same baby doctor. I didn't have to explain anything to him. We were married in 1977.

We lived in Jamestown for several years. I had pictures of Master all over the house. I went to convocation. I even started a little meditation group of local nursing students. I talked about God and the Gurus all the time. He read the *Autobiography*, so he knew about Master's life. He also knew SRF was important to me. He was respectful of everything I did. He didn't question me and he never interfered with my spiritual practice. Never. And he never made me feel I was detracting from our marriage because I was meditating. Because my birth family expected me to be like them, to feel and want what they felt and wanted, I had no expectation he'd follow my path. I never urged him to join SRF. Master was a part of our lives, and he had tremendous respect for him, but that's as far as it went.

We moved to Atlanta in 1983 and I joined the SRF group there. He went to law school. I worked three jobs to get us through until he was hired by a good firm. Then, in 1994, I felt the pull to return to Encinitas. My internal clock said, "It's time to go back." I needed to go "home."

I got a nursing job in Encinitas; he stayed in Atlanta with his law firm. My two oldest children were almost grown so they stayed in Atlanta as well, and I took our youngest daughter to Encinitas. It was a hard parting. He came to Encinitas for birthdays and holidays, and not a day went by when we didn't talk on the phone.

About three years later, he called me up and said, "I want to take the Lessons. It's time." I was glad for him—and a little dumbfounded. I'd been on the path twenty years by then, and neither he nor I had ever said a word about him becoming a member. I knew if SRF was for him, it had to come from within him; it had to mean something to him. I think, now, Master moved me to Encinitas to give him time by himself to develop his own relationship with the guru and become involved at the SRF Atlanta Center on his own without me "translating." He started the Lessons and became an integral part of the group. He moved to Encinitas in 2008, and we are here to stay.

There's a poem etched on my heart that says, in part:

March on child of eternal lightening …
March on with steady steps!
I take these things away from thee
So that thou mayest receive them
From My hands, from Me.

To me, this means God sometimes takes precious things from our lives to eventually return them to us "new and improved," direct from His hands. My husband was a wonderful father and husband when I married him and became, in Master's hands, an even more wonderful husband, father, and devotee. I saw the truth of this poem unfold in our relationship.

When I first read the *Autobiography*, I was beyond blown away. I'd never understood this planet, what we were all doing here or who was running the show. I didn't get the memo. When I read the *Autobiography*, everything made sense. The stories of Master's anguish at his Mother's death and at Sri Yukteswar's death—the depth of his love and his loyalty to them—are so touching to me. When our son died, I knew Master understood what I was feeling. He carried me. I felt Him saying, "You're not going to know anything going into this, but I'm here with you and you're going to be fine."

My relationship with Master is my saving grace. Once you realize who God is, and why He is, and who you are in relation to Him, there's no question about what life is about.

SIX

My Time Had Come

I am the husband referred to in the previous story. Though our beginnings on the path are different, I am greatly blessed to share this remarkable spiritual journey Master has given the world with my wife, my best friend.

I'm seventy years old, also born and raised in Jamestown, brought up in the Lutheran tradition. My mother was a nurse; my father was a blue-collar laborer. They weren't educated people, but they were honest. They didn't swear. They didn't drink, except for a holiday cocktail on Christmas Eve.

My grandmother lived with us and she was the one who took my sister and me to Sunday school almost every Sunday of my childhood. We never talked about God at home. We never prayed together. I probably saw my Dad in church three times the whole time I was growing up. My mother liked to go to church on Easter to see the hats.

The first time I was old enough to go to church on my own and they passed the collection plate, I thought they were giving me a "treat," that it was like Halloween, so I took some of the donation envelopes and put them in my pocket. When I got home I was immediately taken back to church to return the money and apologize to the minister!

I believed in God as a child because this is what I was taught to do in Sunday school and by my grandmother. I thought He was a grand old man who ran everybody's lives and waited for us to come up to heaven, but I had no idea what happened after we got there. As I grew older, I formed my own ideas about things, including God. Nothing in my life had proven to me God existed, so by the time I went away to college I was—like many kids of my generation—an agnostic.

I was the first person in my family to go to college. I went to a small liberal arts school in Indiana, majored in geography, then went to graduate school and got my Master's Degree, also in geography. That was about the time I reconnected with my wife. We had known each other a little bit in junior high school; her stepbrother and I were good friends, but I hadn't seen her for probably fifteen years. I came home from grad school one weekend for a visit, and some friends said, "Guess who's back in town?" They suggested I call her. I did and we started dating.

One of the first conversations we had about SRF was about the meditation armrest known as the Aum Board she'd made when she lived in the woods—two 2"x4"s attached, stained, and upholstered with a piece of fabric. I asked her what it was and she said, "It's what we meditate with." Then I asked, "Do you ever fall off when you sit on it?" What did I know?

She told me about *Autobiography of a Yogi* so I read it. It was an amazing story, but I wasn't drawn to the teachings at the time. We just were starting out our marriage and I was trying to find a meaningful career. After we moved to Atlanta, I went to law school. It was a busy time. She'd say, "I'm going to meditation," and I'd say, "Great." This is how it was for about five years. I never tried to discourage her. I always felt everybody had a right to follow whatever spiritual practice they believed was best for them. I couldn't imagine saying, "Don't go," or "I'm not happy with what you're doing." I knew SRF was an important part of her life, and I would no more have discouraged her involvement with Master than I would have discouraged her from spending time with our children.

When she told me she wanted to move to Encinitas, I was stunned. I thought, what am I going to do if I want to ask her something or tell her something and she's not here? I understood what she wanted to do, and I knew she needed to do what she needed to do. I never felt Master was interfering in my life. But it was hard. It felt like I was losing my best friend. It took me a long time to get used to the idea of her not being with me in Atlanta.

After she'd been in Encinitas a few months, I came for a visit. We went often to the SRF Meditation Gardens, but I didn't go to services. I walked on the beach while she went to Temple. The following year I decided to move to Encinitas. Even then, I didn't have an inkling SRF was my path. I was coming to Encinitas to be with my wife. The first year I was there, I walked on the beach fifty-two straight weekends while she went to Temple!

Over time, I wanted to know more about why SRF was so important to her. If something was this essential to her happiness, I felt I needed to better understand it. I started to go by myself to Thursday night services. I really liked the *satsangs*, and hearing the different minister's perspectives on the teachings. It was intellectually refreshing to hear I was not going to go to hell! I also really liked the atmosphere of the Temple on Thursday evenings. I began to seriously think, then, about joining SRF.

I was in Encinitas for about two years when I got a call from a friend in Atlanta, an older attorney who was retiring, and wanted to know if I'd be interested in taking over his law practice. It was a great opportunity. My wife and I talked about my returning to Atlanta and we decided I'd try it for a year. Right after I settled in from the move, something inside me said, "Take the Lessons." I called my wife and said, "I think I'd like to take the Lessons." It was 1997. We had been married twenty years and all the while, not a word passed between us about my joining SRF. But there it was. My time had come.

I remember being excited when my first lesson arrived. The Atlanta Meditation Center was meeting in an office park then, and I thought I should probably go over there and check things out, but I was so busy with the law practice I didn't get to it. Some months later, my wife came for a visit and introduced me to some of the people from the Center. Still, I didn't get involved for several years. I just studied the Lessons and meditated on my own as I always had.

Four years later, in 2001, I took a leave of absence from work to hike the Appalachian Trail with a friend. When I came back, the Kriya Lessons were waiting for me. I was learning many important things from Master's teachings, and I knew he was my guru, so taking Kriya felt like a very natural progression for me. I got my Kriya from Mukti Mata at Mother Center that year.

About five years later, I was talking with my wife on the phone and she said, "You need to get yourself over to the Atlanta Center!" It was one of the best pieces of advice she ever gave me. The following Sunday I walked into the Center and felt like I'd belonged there for years. This was, to me, the ultimate definition of the SRF family. They were so welcoming I wanted to go back.

I'm the studious type, a book learner. I'm not a naturally devotional or social person. Even now, I much prefer to sit quietly in the back of the chapel because Master said he would return to the earth one day and sit in the back of the Temple. I want to be there when he comes. But the experience of being with other devotees added a new, heart-felt dimension to my spiritual life I hadn't known existed. I started going to group meditations, I started to volunteer—to clean or do whatever I could to be of service. When they put me to work in the Bookroom, I felt very much at home.

When I returned to Encinitas in 2011, I was no longer a Sunday morning beach walker. I knew Master was guiding me. His teachings had made such a positive impact on my life, on how I lived my life—more so than if I had not been his devotee. I *wanted* to go to the services. I *wanted* to volunteer. I *wanted* to clean the Sunday school on Saturday mornings. I feel thankful for everything he's given me—then and now—and I want to give back as much as I can.

If you are raised in other churches, you are told that Judgment Day is coming and you either will go "here" or "there." Master knew so many people and he never judged them. Despite all the things we do or don't do, our guru does not judge us. All he says is, "Pick yourself up and start again. Try again." So, I keep trying. I don't have to go back to Square One each time, but when I get a little lax, I just get serious and—with his help—I try again. He has helped me become a better person and I am very grateful for that.

The story Master tells in one of the last chapters of *Autobiography of a Yogi* about giving Mr. Dickinson the silver chalice as a Christmas gift really touches my heart. Mr. Dickinson tells Master about meeting Swami Vivekananda as a seventeen-year-old boy in Chicago and wondering if he was his guru. Vivekananda tells him, "Your teacher will come later. He will give you a silver cup. He will pour out to you more blessings than you are now able to hold." Mr. Dickinson had to wait forty-three years for this to happen, but it did, and exactly as Vivekananda said it would.

This story brings the spiritual life to a human level I really understand. It proves to me that what a man of God-realization says is true; that what he promises *will* come to pass. Even though Mr. Dickinson had to wait decades for that silver chalice, his story gives me hope and fills me with awe. It's like a Hallmark Christmas card with a sweet ending that makes you cry. It opened my heart. It took two avatars to do it, but it proved to me that everything Master says is true. I'm a believer.

SEVEN

An Embarrassment of Riches

I'm a single mother with three kids. I work as a physician's assistant in San Diego. I was born forty-eight years ago in Israel and lived on a kibbutz for the first thirteen years of my life.

My mom is from Minneapolis. She went to Israel when she was eighteen, married my father, and had four children. She's bright and well educated. My dad is from Morocco. He also left home as a young man. He couldn't read or write when they married and was raised in a very misogynistic family. Their relationship was abusive and chaotic from the word "go."

Living on a kibbutz is a collective experience rooted in the philosophies of socialism and Zionism. Child-rearing was done by members of the collective. I spent only a few hours a day with my parents. The Bible was the core text of my education, taught from a historical rather than spiritual perspective, as though everything actually happened. Preserving Jewish identity was more important than having a relationship with God. When a child was eighteen, they enlisted in the army. Parents gave their sons and daughters to the military to fight in the name of Israel. Having a child in the army was a great source of pride for Israeli parents.

Despite this indoctrination, I had a secret relationship with God. I remember lying in bed at night and talking with God. Not the Old Testament God I learned about in school that, in my opinion, had serious anger management issues, but with a God who was my friend; someone I'd tell stories to and ask questions of. As my "education" progressed, that God faded and my consciousness became more attached to the fire, brimstone, floods, turn-you-into-a-pillar-of-salt God I heard about in school that always punished you when you stepped out of line. This was not a God I wanted to be close to. How can you feel safe with a God like that, particularly as a child?

We returned to Minneapolis when I was thirteen because my dad believed streets in America were paved with gold and we would make our fortune there. That was not the case. Their marriage, our life, became more chaotic and abusive. Three years later, they divorced.

Given what I witnessed in my parents' relationship, I started creating my own chaos early on. By the time I was fifteen, I was drinking and boy crazy, getting into my own violent relationships. I got sober at nineteen and attempted to create a relationship with the God I encountered in the 12-Step Program, a nondenominational God who is loving and forgiving. But I was a stranger to that God. My AA sponsor told me to get on my knees every morning and say, "God, please keep me sober," and get back on my knees at night and say, "Thank You for keeping me safe." I'd never prayed like that before. It wasn't something I knew how to do. It was uncomfortable to talk like that to a God I wasn't sure loved me.

One night, it was so painful to be in my skin, I got down on my knees and said, "If You want me to stay here, You have got to *do* something!" And for an instant, Something met my words. I felt it. I knew it. Then It was gone. But It was enough. From then on I started reciting St. Francis of Assisi's beautiful "Lord, make me an instrument of your peace." I went to synagogue. I followed the rules. I attempted to engage God.

I married when I was twenty-five. I wanted a relationship different from what my parents had. He was a law student; I was getting my degree in genetics and cell biology. He was Jewish; I was Jewish. He was an immigrant; I was an immigrant. It looked good on paper. Long story short, there was a lot of emotional abuse in my marriage.

Judaism encourages intellectual questioning, but not questioning that asks for solutions to what you don't understand. Why violence? Why emotional abuse? Why suffering? In Israel, Judaism is about pride that you survived. Even if there's suffering, even when you don't understand, you follow the rules. I wanted my Judaism to appease God because I needed to make sure the God I knew about didn't get angry with me. I tried to create a model of what a healthy relationship and a loving Jewish home should be, but I didn't know how to do that. Did God care more about whether I ate pork or whether I was mean? I didn't know what the rules meant or what they had to do with real life or how following them would get me closer to God, so there was a lot of whistling in the dark.

When my children were born I realized, "Okay, I'm playing for keeps now." Parenthood was the homing signal that pulled me toward creating a deeper connection with God. I put my kids in Jewish preschools and tried to make who I was and the relationship I wanted with God fit that external paradigm. But I was always afraid of what the God I learned about as a child would take from me because that's what God supposedly did to the Jewish people. I was certain I deserved punishment so I never relaxed into the relationship. As my marriage grew worse, my pull towards God grew very strong. I remember saying, "What do You want from me? I'm trying my best!" I was giving God a soul call.

Within the year, a Jewish girlfriend introduced me to a little, round, white-haired woman who taught a form of meditation where you memorized a passage from whatever liturgical text appealed to you and walked that prayer at a steady cadence. That my friend was a "respectable Jewish girl" allowed me to take this class without feeling I was going outside my faith. This teacher introduced me to the

Autobiography. "If you're interested in learning more about meditation," she said, "here's an interesting book." I remembered Master's face on the cover, but the thought of reading anything was way beyond what I had time for with three young kids and a busy career.

About a year later, a patient came into the clinic where I worked for a breast exam—she thought she had a lump—and there was something unusually peaceful about her. She didn't seem anxious like women are in that circumstance. As I did the exam, I said, "If you don't mind me saying, you seem very calm." And she said, "That's because I have a guru."

I say, "You have a guru!"

She says, "Yes. I have a guru."

She went on to mention the *Autobiography*, and I said, "I've heard of that book."

She said, "If you don't mind, I'd love to give it to you. I'll bring it on my next visit." I told her okay and she left.

After she'd gone, I remembered I was about to start a new job in another department and she wouldn't be able to get me the book when she returned for her next visit. So I did something I'd never done and called her up. After work, I drove to Encinitas. She gave me the *Autobiography* and started telling me about the miracle that is Master. I'm very drawn! There's something there, I know it! And I got the sense this would change everything!

I'm dyslexic and reading is challenging, so I didn't read the book for a few weeks. Finally, I got the audio book at the SRF bookstore read by Sir Ben Kingsley. The whole experience was pretty revolutionary! Like, "Come on! *Really*? Are you *sure*?"

Now the battle for my soul began. The God I knew had to die, and false gods don't *like* to die. They fight. Hard! But now I knew the Truth, so I fought hard for my soul! My husband was not okay with what I was doing. He didn't want the kids to see me meditate, so I meditated in my closet before they woke up and after they went to sleep. I couldn't have an altar, so a little statue of a golden frog sitting in meditation that was given to me by my former mediation teacher became my altar. I wrestled with going to a temple where Jesus was on the altar, but I continued meeting my patient and listened to her talk about God and Guru. And I loved it all! Eventually, she gave me some CDs by the monastics. Listening to them I felt I'd come home. I had *finally* come home. I thought, if *this* is God, I'm in! A God that loves me and talks to me, and wants a relationship with me? Yes, please.

Finally, I talked with a minister who told me the most important thing was for me to meditate. "The answers will become clear to you then," he said. He was right. I started to come to Temple. I signed up for the SRF Lessons, and over the next few years, it became clear SRF was my path and Master was the real deal.

Then one day, I was overcome by doubt. I was stopped at a light on a little bridge and noticed a man sitting on the bridge with a great smile on his face waving to everybody in their cars. He pointed to me, smiled, then sat in meditation posture. I knew in my heart that somehow God put him there to show me I was on the right track. So I said to God, "You would arrange the universe and put that happy man there at exactly the moment I stopped for the light just because I needed help?" Until that point, my predominant understanding of God was still that He was angry with me, and that I needed to be punished. But in that moment, I realized I'm special! And I'm His! Though I knew I'd continue to struggle to love God and know God's love, I would no longer question SRF was my path.

I still tried to make my marriage work according to Master's guidance, but things got worse. Eventually I found the courage to leave him. God and Guru took me by the hand and got me through.

I made the commitment to raise my children Jewish when they were born and I continue to do that. Once they are bar mitzvah, they are adults in the eyes of the Jewish people. If they then want to be on another path, that's up to them. I give them the notes and they make whatever music they want. I practice Master's teachings. I do my Kriya. I still struggle with negative self-talk, but my sense of being loved by God has grown 100% and I feel God loves me in my atoms. That's what I want for my kids. I do not want them to have the paucity consciousness I grew up with.

Sri Yukteswar tells the story in *Autobiography of a Yogi* about how his mother told him there were ghosts in a dark chamber in their house, so he went to that very place and proved to his mother there were no ghosts there. "Look fear in the face and it will cease to trouble you," he said. He also said, "Forget the past. The vanished lives of all men are dark with many shames. Human conduct is ever unreliable until man is anchored in the Divine. Everything in future will improve if you are making a spiritual effort now." I can face anything now. It doesn't mean I don't get scared. It doesn't mean I don't fall into old patterns or old habits, but I know now, with every fiber of my being, that I am loved and I am His.

If the only help I get for the rest of my life is what I've gotten up to this moment, it's more than I will ever need for my lifetime. I have Guru. I have the teachings. I can pray. I can meditate. It's an embarrassment of riches. Truly.

EIGHT

Mother, I Give You My Soul

I'm sixty-two, born in Columbus, Ohio, four days after Sputnik was launched. One of the first Space Age babies. Middle America. Middle class. My father was a lawyer. My mother was a social worker. They were high fiber, moral people. No stealing. No carousing. "Behave according to our rules if you're going to live under this roof." They had their foibles, but they were good parents.

When I was a kid, they dressed me up in a little suit and sent me down to Sunday school at the local Methodist church while they stayed home, read the paper, and ate pastries. I wanted to stay home and eat pastries, too, but they felt it was important I have some sort of moral and religious training so I went to Sunday school until the sixth grade. As I remember it, they chose this church because it was the closest one to our house. I don't remember what I learned there with any particular fondness, or that what I learned had any real impact on how I lived my life, but it did plant the seeds for my spiritual unfoldment later on.

I have one brother, three years older than I am, who was an iconoclastic atheist kind of guy. He's now a Tibetan Buddhist. He left home at seventeen and ended up in Colorado.

My parents didn't talk about God when I was growing up. My mother referred to my father as a deist, sort of like Thomas Jefferson. My dad believed in a Higher Power that created the universe, but he did not believe that life continued after death. My mother was close to the vest about her religious beliefs. She was raised in a Hungarian family of Catholics and Lutherans. Hungarians are fun people. They celebrate holidays with lots of laughter and joy. When she was growing up, she and her siblings were always involved in church activities and pageants. She had some spiritual experiences later in life, and I realized what an old soul she was, but she was not interested in pursuing anything overtly spiritual.

When I was thirteen, my brother somehow got hold of *Autobiography of a Yogi* and I read it. I'd read a little of the Bible by then, and it bugged me that spiritual experiences only seemed to happen to people 2000 years ago. Why not now, I wondered? When I read the *Autobiography,* I was glad to know these things were still going on, but I was thirteen, and I was immature; I wasn't ready for the teachings. So I put the *Autobiography* aside, then got into lots of trouble drinking and doing drugs and carousing—enough trouble to realize I needed to clean up my act!

I was twenty before I wised up. I began reading the Bible again and talked to a neighbor who took me to his Baptist church. I got baptized—the full immersion—and invited all my party friends to the baptism to send them the message that I was done partying. None of them came except for one girl. I started going to a Christian church and a young adults class, but it just wasn't enough for me. It was like the blind leading the blind—sincere, well intentioned people who just didn't have the kind of direct, personal experience I was looking for. So I left Ohio "to see America" and went to visit my brother in Colorado. He had the *Autobiography* in his house, and this time when I read it, that was it! I signed up for the SRF Lessons and began going to the weekly meditation at the Boulder Meditation Group.

About nine months later, I also began attending Sunday services at the Unity Church because the SRF group didn't meet on Sunday. I met a guy there who had a farm on the western slope of Colorado and a group of us from Unity drove out and spent the weekend there. I remember writing in my *Spiritual Diary* that night, "Wouldn't it be great to live in a spiritual community on a farm?" and within a month, I got an unsolicited phone call from the Boulder Meditation Group leader telling me about a guy who needed his car driven to California, all expenses paid, to an ashram SRF was starting in Hidden Valley. It was as if Master had read my diary and said, "Okay! This guy's ready! Call him up!" I hadn't been to convocation yet, and I really wanted to go that year, so a buddy and I drove this car out to Hidden Valley. I ended up living there—on a farm, in a spiritual community—for fifteen months!

In his book *The Divine Romance*, Master speaks of friends from past lives as "friends once more to be." Brother Dharmananda and the men I served with at Hidden Valley were such friends to me. Brother was "the rock." He worked hard and was a straight shooter who didn't mince words. He was a great guy, and a true mentor to me. I lived in a semi-cloistered environment with like-minded individuals all pointed in the same direction, all of us working hard together for Master. I got thoroughly inculcated in Master's teachings. It was one of the most special times of my life.

Being there was very appealing, but attractive as it was, I knew I wasn't going to be a monk; I knew I had too many desires. Once I realized this, I needed to decide what I *did* want to do with my life, then move forward with that decision: get a job, go to church, work and live in the devotee community. My time at Hidden Valley was Master's doing and his blessing. I needed to grow up a bit and he knew that; the karma was right for me to go there and then it was right for me to move on. The hand of God was at work and I knew Master was guiding me.

A lot of people know what they want to do with their lives when they're a kid, but that wasn't me. I took a career interest inventory test to match my interests and skills to a profession I'd enjoy and be good at. Physical Therapy was one of the things that came up. I started volunteering at a PT clinic and really liked it, so six years after high school, I went back to college. I moved to Encinitas and lived with a bunch of SRF guys while I was in school. We were really tight, and we've remained life-long friends. In 1987, I graduated college with a degree in physical therapy and married my wife all in the same month. We've been married thirty-two years. She's one of the best things that ever happened to me.

I'm incredibly fortunate now to live near a temple, to have a hive of serious seekers around me. We talk about what we're learning, we learn from each other, and there's a lot of support for what we're trying to overcome. Spiritual friendship is, itself, a spiritual environment, a current we all swim in that moves us in the same direction.

I've had a thirty-two year career as a physical therapist. It was a fabulous choice for me. I did good work and made a lot of money. And it was fun! But that's not my focus now. I've just gone through a serious health challenge where I had to get to the point where I could let go of everything and be able to say that what I really want now is Divine Mother's will. I went back to work after my treatment— just to prove to myself I could do it—but I'm learning more deeply that whatever She wants is fabulous! My prayer to Her now is, "Keep me on the planet so I can do *sadhana*. If You take me, great, but if that's what You want, You've got to promise to bring me back to the core group of devotees who serve Your work." I don't want to be a goat farmer out in the middle of Tajikistan by myself. I want to be as close to the inner circle of Paramahansaji's work as I can get, with devotees who are seeking and serving God.

Most of my life I just stumbled along unconsciously as my karma ripened and different opportunities presented themselves. Divine Mother and Master led me to Hidden Valley, to my career, and to my wife and friends pretty much without my knowing. I look back on my life now and see blessing after blessing, opportunity after opportunity. I understand that Divine Mother knows what I need and provides the right opportunities for me at the right time. I just need to pay attention and move forward. If I don't pay attention, I miss the lessons I could learn and the opportunities that come to me. I'm one of Master's people, so he takes care of me. I'm so relieved to realize I'm not in charge.

Sure, we have our karma, we attract opportunities and blessings into our lives, but I'm not in charge of the whole show; Divine Mother and Master are. I'm being led now to what's next, and I want to consciously be more aware of what She's doing in my life so I can cooperate with and surrender to Her plan. Given what I've been through, I'm just trying to show up and say, "Well, what are we doing today, Mother?" I pray for God's will for me, and prefer others do the same because that's what moves the Mother most.

If I plan things on my own, my life would be much worse than it is. She's given me way more than I think I deserve or desired or even knew was possible. That gives me great faith in Divine Mother. I'm so grateful.

I once heard a story about a man who knew Master who had a sudden desire for a new car. He goes right out and buys a nice car and drives over to show it off to Master. Master looks at the car and smiles, then says, "If you had just let that desire go, Divine Mother would have given you a Cadillac." God's prepared to give us a lot more than what we think we need or deserve. If we get out of Her way, really great stuff happens.

When I was seven, I saw a documentary about yogis who were buried in the sand, then dug up and found alive. I thought, when I grow up, I want to be a yogi, though I had no idea what that actually meant. In the time I have left, I want to take care of my wife, be at the Temple, and get in some serious *sadhana*. I want to be a yogi.

One of my favorite quotes in the *Autobiography* is from Sri Yukteswar: "Forget the past. The vanished lives of all men are dark with many shames. Human conduct is ever unreliable until man is anchored in the Divine. Everything in future will improve if you are making the spiritual effort now." This gives me great solace.

I've heard it said that eventually, Divine Mother brings everyone to their knees. Sooner or later, everybody has to show up. All I'm in charge of is loving God. The more I let go and do that, the more I feel powerless and powerful at the same time.

I also like the passage from *God Talks With Arjuna: The Bhagavad Gita*, where Krishna says to Arjuna, "O Partha, surrender not to unmanliness; it is unbecoming to thee. O Scorcher of Foes, forsake this small weak hearted-ness! Arise!" That's the battle cry of my soul. When I have those thoughts, I feel powerful.

NINE

His Invisible Arms

I was born in Austin, Texas, the oldest of three girls, thirty-four years ago, but I grew up in Orange County, California. I'm Vietnamese. My dad was afraid my sisters and I wouldn't assimilate so he only spoke English to us. My mom wanted us to retain our Vietnamese heritage so she only spoke Vietnamese to us. Right from the start, I had a foot in two different worlds.

I grew up in a spiritual environment. My dad is very spiritual even though he's an agnostic. My mom was born Buddhist and Tao, but was always searching. My sisters and I made offerings to all the buddhas and to our ancestors at our family altar, especially my grandpa and great-grandmother, and we went with my mom to Christian churches, Lutheran churches, Catholic churches, Tao Holy Houses, and various Buddhist temples. I also attended a Mormon temple for a while on my own. Though my mom eventually returned to her Buddhist roots, I ended up feeling like I didn't belong anywhere. Other girls my age would carry around pretty little Precious Moments bibles at the churches we went to and I dreamed of being included in their group, but they didn't want to be friends with me.

This idea of not knowing where I fit and wanting to belong was embedded into my childhood in other ways, too. Orange County has the largest Vietnamese population outside of Vietnam in the world; Vietnamese markets, shops, and restaurants are everywhere. Garden Grove, where we lived, is not as affluent as other parts of Orange County, but the kids dressed "ghetto fabulous"—very street cool—and talked in an improvised slang that was part Vietnamese and part English. I wanted to please my parents and sound educated, so my peers made fun of the way I talked and told me I sounded like a white girl. It was another disconnect. I didn't feel Vietnamese enough, and I didn't feel American enough. I was also born with a spinal disease and had three back surgeries before I was nineteen, so part of me was uncomfortable just being in my body.

When I was about seven, I began to have a relationship with God that was not dependent on anything or anyone outside myself. Each night, for a moment before I fell asleep, it was just me and God. I didn't know how to ask Him for anything, or even that I could tell Him my problems, so I talked to Buddha and Kwan Yen—my home Goddess, the ultimate Vietnamese expression of Divine Mother—because they were already part of my life. Mostly,

I just repeated Kwan Yen's mantra in my head: *Nam mo quan the am bo tat.* (I bow to the Goddess of Compassion, Quan Yin.) The root words of this mantra are Sanskrit. Though I didn't realize it then, India was in the background of my mind very early in my life.

When I was sixteen, I went to a performing arts high school and started taking acting classes, then went into the acting program at Cal State, Fullerton. Acting helped me feel confident and break out of my shell. After graduation I did everything I could to enter the industry. I tried so hard I burned myself out. I had some mild success: a few commercials, a few music videos, a few indie films. Now, like every aspiring actor in L.A., I do many things: I teach yoga, I'm an assistant to a film producer, and I occasionally narrate audio books. I just want to use my God-given talents to serve the world in whatever way Guruji wants to use me.

Hatha Yoga became a big part of my life in my last year of college. My body was stiff from all the surgery and, by the grace of God, the owner of the yoga studio I went to was a chiropractor and a physical therapist. With his help, the postures helped me connect with my body. One day, a friend invited me to another studio that happened to be owned by devotees. Guruji's picture was on the wall. When I first saw him, I thought, as many people do, that he was a woman.

Though I didn't connect to him then, the instructor led a meditation at the end of class that made a lasting impression on me. "Imagine," he said, "that the love in your heart is expanding throughout your entire body, then throughout the room, throughout the city, then all of California, the United States, the world, the universe." I dropped into my soul and, for the first time in my life, I was at total peace with who I am. Nine years later, when I began the SRF Lessons, I recognized that meditation in one of the Lessons, and understood Guruji was with me long before I understood who he was.

After that experience, I was hooked on yoga. I took teacher training and learned yoga philosophy and the Sanskrit names for the poses. Later that year, a friend took me to the SRF Lake Shrine Temple in the Pacific Palisades and I again saw Master's picture. I was now very curious about him, but I was still not ready for the path. Over the course of five years, I went from yoga studio to yoga studio looking for where I belonged. I even lived in an ashram in Colorado for six months. Every day we'd chant the *Guru Gita* and do *arti pujas*—ceremonies of Light—to the Hindu gods and goddesses, but it wasn't "home" and I knew it, so I left.

When I returned to L.A., I made a friend who lived next door to the Lake Shrine Temple. We'd often walk around the grounds. It was very peaceful. One night, she invited me to a commemoration service honoring Lahiri Mahasaya. It was interesting to me, but I still didn't connect.

About a year later, I was sitting at a friend's desk reading and I felt someone looking at me. I looked up and saw Guruji's face on a bookmark poking out of a book on the shelf behind me. A week later, I was in a vegetarian restaurant in Hollywood and, once again, I felt his presence. I turned around and discovered Guruji's picture hanging on the wall behind me. I thought, "Wow! Yogananda is following me!" These kinds of experiences kept happening, and it got so I couldn't stop thinking about him.

Though I was not yet a devotee, I began going to Sunday morning services at the Lake Shrine. I was in pretty bad shape financially then—no job, no home, no resources—but based on the trust I was beginning to develop in Master, I started doing the affirmations on the SRF Horn of Plenty Bank. A few days later, someone gave me some beautifully framed pictures of all the gurus. I had a full altar gifted to me while I was saying Master's abundance affirmations, and I realized these pictures were the spiritual abundance I always longed for. A few weeks later, I also got work and booked a big commercial.

I didn't know anyone at the Lake Shrine, but I kept going to Sunday service because I loved it so much. Sometimes I'd go to the first service then stay for the second service because I needed to hear what the minister said a second time. Then one Sunday, they announced there would be a Young Adults meeting after the monthly Friendship Tea. Meeting others my age that were seeking God on this path connected me, for the first time in my life, to a community that supported my spiritual life.

I started going regularly to Young Adult meetings and signed up for the SRF Lessons. A solid year of practicing the meditation techniques and being with spiritual friends helped me see who Master really is. When I finally read the *Autobiography*, I not only learned where Guruji comes from, I understood where *I* come from as well, that my connection to yoga—and to him—went beyond this lifetime. In *Songs of the Soul*, Master says to his devotees, "Unknown I will walk by your side, And guard you with invisible arms." As difficult as my life had been, I now understood I was always being guided and guarded. My challenges were blessings in disguise that brought me back to him. He never forgot me, life after life; *I* just had to remember who I am. Reading the *Autobiography* was like the cherry on top of the sundae of my entire life. This is *it* for me, I thought. Forever and forever. I'm done looking. I'm home.

I've always felt very Indian. During my time at the ashram in Colorado, I was exposed to many aspects of Indian culture, including meditation. But taking Kriya made all the difference in my spiritual life, like nothing else I've ever done. It anchored me, anchored my devotion. My meditations got better. They got easier. They got deeper. And my desire for meditation increased. I used to think an hour meditation was all I could do. Now I enjoy longer meditations.

A lot of "stuff" came up when I took Kriya—things I had to work out—but that's okay. Guruji "means business!" He wants me to be the best version of my Self, and every day I pray to him to help me be that Self.

He's also more tangible with Kriya. He shows me in unexpected ways he's by my side. One morning last October

I had a strong desire to visit Mother Center. I wanted to meditate in the chapel and offer a challenge I was having to Master. As I was meditating, I began to hear the monastics chanting "Jai Guru." I walked into the reception area to see what was happening at the exact moment Brother Chidananda came downstairs from Master's shrine. I didn't know it, but that was the day he left on a pilgrimage to India. As he walked outside, he glanced at me and his *darshan* was full of Master's love. I knew this was Master telling me I'd be okay.

I've thought about being a nun, but I don't feel that's my path this life. Guruji is leading my life. If monastic life *is* meant for me, he will let me know. Then nothing would stop me from doing that.

The biggest thing I've learned since coming to the path is that I don't really know anything. That's a big relief! It's easy to be judgmental, to think someone is not spiritual because they're doing this or not being that. When you live in a spiritual community you see both sides of the coin because we live in duality.

Master says in *Inner Peace,* "You have come on earth to entertain and be entertained." To me, this means not to expect lasting happiness and perfection from anyone or anything except God and Guru, and not to take what happens so seriously. I surrender myself at his lotus feet. The teachings help me be honest with myself and with God. I look at Guruji's picture and I tell him the truth about what's going on in my life and how I'm feeling. Then I don't have anything to hide. I'm not perfect at this. I don't do it well every time, but I go to him and he gives me shelter. The Sanskrit word is *sharanam*. Having Master makes all the difference in my life. This is where I belong. This is how I belong. And Master is who I belong to. I'm home.

TEN

Leaning on the Lord

I'm fifty-seven years old, married with one son, and an attorney. I came from a family of eight, born and raised in North Carolina in the Bible Belt. My father was a long-distance truck driver with a ninth grade education; my mother worked in a textile mill for as long as her health permitted.

My mother was ill when I was coming up and passed away when I was thirteen. Dad was always on the road. The older kids watched the younger kids and everybody pulled their weight. There was too much riding on keeping the family together for any of us to get into any trouble, so we were all pretty well behaved. It was tough times.

There are all kinds of ironies involved in growing up African-American in a town where children sometimes cannot go to the Christmas parade because the Ku Klux Klan is marching in the parade. I understood early on that if I were ever going to go to college, I'd be leaning on the Lord to get there. Through His grace, the adversity of my childhood became the canvas He used to paint my life with hope and possibility, and I was led to two English teachers with profound love in their hearts that took an interest in my development as a student and supported me in ways I find hard to express in words.

There's a church on every other block in the Bible Belt, and everyone you know goes to church on Sundays. Everything in your life is church, so it feels like you're before the Lord 24/7. One of my earliest memories is of my mother telling me Jesus was my friend. The whole sky opened up when she said that. I walked outside afterward and it was sunny and I was so happy I'd recollected my Friend. I've talked to him with that kind of familiarity ever since, and I think of him as my "Big Brother."

Our family attended the Church of Christ. They are Fundamentalist—downright Amish in their simplicity—and take Scripture very literally. I knew there was more to the story than what I heard in church because, in our family, there was a thin veil between this world and the next. Several of my relatives were in regular contact with friends and family on the other side. This wasn't everybody's normal, but it was our normal. Had the church known about this, they would have said what we were doing was evil. But I knew what I heard in church was not the whole Truth because my personal experience was bigger than what the Church was teaching.

Big Brother Jesus was my guiding light. I prayed to him to know the truth and asked him to use me as an instrument of his peace. I thought I had a calling to the ministry. The ironic thing is that I'd already decided to be a lawyer in the second grade because I dearly loved my mother and wanted to make her proud. In my senior year in college, I talked with several ministers who helped me see I didn't have to wear a collar to be used by God.

I feel an intuitional resonance when there's something Spirit wants me to do. It doesn't matter if what I'm told to do is contrary to every thought I've ever had, I do what I'm told. I've not always done that right away, however, and I've had a time or two when I thought, Really? *This* is what You want me to do? But I've learned to trust what He tells me. I have faith that all things work together for the greater good, and I do my best to live according to His purpose for me.

This is how I came to Master. In 1991, after I graduated law school, I went to work for the law firm chosen by the government of India to represent their case against Union Carbide after a gas explosion in Bhopal, India injured and killed thousands of people there. The suit was filed in this country because Union Carbide's headquarters were in the U.S.

The attorney general of India came to the U.S. for a status report and sat in on our meetings. He was a devout Hindu—a simple man, very disciplined. He radiated goodness. When everybody went to dinner together after work, he'd take his leave and go to his room to meditate. Though

I knew Jesus, I knew I didn't know what this man knew. I felt the fruits of his knowing and I wondered what kind of spiritual understanding and practice could bring about such a flowering in a man. One night after work, I went to dinner at an Indian restaurant and noticed *Autobiography of a Yogi* in a book section in the restaurant. I'd always wondered what a yogi did and thought this book might also give me some insight into the attorney general, so I bought the book.

I read the *Autobiography* in two days and it resonated within me as the Truth about Spirit and creation. So I asked my Big Brother if I was supposed to follow this path. Right away I'm told, "Sign up for the SRF Lessons." Though I felt that inner resonance, the *Autobiography* was so exotic, so different than what I'd grown up with in the Bible Belt, I hesitated.

I'm always open to my own capacity for delusion, so I wanted confirmation this was the path Jesus wanted me to pursue. I said, "I love you, Jesus, and I love my Heavenly Father, but you have a blind child in me. Have a little mercy here and help me see the Truth."

The next day I got a call from an ex-girlfriend I hadn't talked to in a decade. She told me she was living in L.A. I asked why, and she said she was now a member of Self-Realization Fellowship. This was an interesting coincidence, but I still didn't sign up for the Lessons. Then a few days later, I'm told to go to California and do my signing up in person. I'm still hesitant, but I said, "Okay, I'll go, but

I won't ask for directions to any place when I'm there." I figured if I totally put myself in Jesus' hands and I got where he said I should go, I'd know he was guiding my every turn.

I bought a plane ticket to L.A.X. and flew out the following Sunday. I knew about Encinitas from reading the *Autobiography*, but I'd never been south of L.A. and had no idea where Encinitas was. I just got in a rental car and drove south. After a few hours, I saw a sign on the freeway for Encinitas. I'm like, "Wow! What do you know!" I got off the freeway, turned where I was told to turn, and pulled right up to the SRF Meditation Gardens. I walked through the gates and immediately felt it was hallowed ground.

I stayed the night in a nearby hotel and the next morning I'm told, "Drive to Mother Center"—SRF's international headquarters. I had no clue where it was, except that it was near L.A. I "turn here, turn there," for two hours and got off the freeway when I saw a sign that said, "Welcome to Mount Washington"—the hilltop community I knew from reading the *Autobiography* that was home to SRF headquarters. "Turn here. Go up this hill. Turn there," and I pulled right up to Mother Center.

I got out of the car and saw a sign on the gate saying the grounds were closed Mondays. I thought it was crazy to drive all this way only to find Mother Center was closed, so I started complaining to Jesus about it. As soon as I got back in the car he said, "You didn't do what I told you. Go back to the gate." As I'm walking up to the gate, I see a nun coming towards me down the driveway. I waved. She waved back and asked in her nunly voice if she could help me. I told her I wanted to sign up for the Lessons and she said, "I can help you with that." That's that. So I thought.

As soon as I get back in the car, I'm told to go to Master's crypt at Forest Lawn cemetery. I do *not* want to go there! No thank you! Given my childhood experiences with visitors from the other side, the last place I want to go is someplace where these folks might take an interest in me. My "Helper" starts giving me directions to what I thought was L.A.X., but pretty soon I'm at Forest Lawn. I'm terrified, but decide to pay my respects then leave. After several false starts, I found Master's crypt and sat down on a nearby bench. The peace, the total absence of fear and anxiety, overwhelmed me. As I stood to leave, Spirit gave me the moral to this story: "If you're going to be serious about the spiritual path, you must never fear spiritual things because you are one with the Spirit of all spirits." I flew home, began receiving the Lessons, and I loved them.

You'd think, after that, I'd be set for life. But I still had something to learn. I was studying the Lessons on my own and not yet part of a group. I didn't even know how to pronounce the gurus names. About a year later, I'm back in California, driving Route 1 near Olema, giving Master the business, complaining that though I love the Lessons, I want to meet a living guru. "After all," I said to him, "You had a living guru and I want one, too."

Next thing I knew I saw a sign that said "Vedanta Retreat," and am told to get off the freeway and park in front of a stately old farmhouse with a lot of cars out front. I'm told to go in, but the gate is locked, so I climbed the fence, walked to the back porch and peeked in. A man motioned to me to join several people sitting in a circle inside the house. As I enter the room, the group is discussing *Autobiography of a Yogi,* and I hear, for the first time, my gurus names pronounced aloud. Someone asked why I'd come to the meeting. I told them I'm a Lessons student and wanted a living guru. They point to an old Indian fellow sitting in the circle and tell me he's their guru, then he looks at me and tells me that he's not accepting new students, but he'll accept me because I've been sent there. By then, it's clear to me how alive Master is! I thanked them for their hospitality and left. That set my foot on the path for good. I got my Kriya in 1994 and started to serve the work.

Master's teachings provide a knowing that allows me to spiritually exhale, to say "Yes!" to the truth of who I am—who we all are—and to the Oneness behind all true religions. He's like a mountain—so grand—yet so familiar, so human. Such a sense of humor! Omnipresence and love! I have "test days;" I get "pop quizzes" and he lays it on thick to see how I react. But when something exciting happens, my first thought is to tell him.

In *The Divine Romance*, Master says, "Sometimes I am more with you in God when I am away than when I am with you personally." Reading the *Autobiography* gives life to these consoling words. I discover the transcendent truth about our guru, about all the SRF gurus. They are not characters in a book. They are living and active in *all* our lives, enlightened beings that walk with us and talk with us because we are their own. To have the consciousness that hears and receives everything all your devotees say—our urges, our wishes, our needs, our prayers—I can't conceive it! To have a guru like that! To have this path! It's such a blessing.

ELEVEN

A Living Presence

I'm an only child, born in 1943 in Austin, Texas. My parents were geologists. We moved to Buenos Aires when I was six months old and lived there four years until my parents divorced. My mother and I returned to Texas and she eventually married an old friend from college, also a geologist. The three of us moved to Denver, Colorado in 1949.

My parents were raised as Methodists. My stepfather loved to go to church. He was a jazz musician as well as a scientist, and he loved gospel music. My mother didn't believe in anything that couldn't be scientifically proven—including God—but she accompanied my father to church while I went to Sunday school.

I was deeply attracted to the ideals of service and world brotherhood I learned about in Sunday school. I heard about Albert Schweitzer's work and wanted to go to Africa to help him and became fascinated by a UNICEF children dressed in the clothing of various cultures holding hands around the Earth. That image of world brotherhood was implanted in my heart and has never left me.

Both my parents loved Nature. It was a deep source of joy for them, and we spent many happy hours together picnicking in the mountains and looking for fossils and crystals. As an only child, I was frequently by myself, lying in the mountain fields communing with the clouds and the flowers. God as Nature became my dearest friend and companion.

Then, when I was nine, my Sunday school teacher asked my class if any of us had spoken to God. I confidently raised my hand and said, "I've talked to God." She got very angry with me and accused me of showing off. "Nobody can talk to God," she said. I thought she was right because she was the teacher, but I was bereft. I felt like I lost my best friend. I stopped talking to God until I found Master.

We moved to the other side of town when I was fifteen and stopped going to church because it was too far away from where we lived. The first Christmas Eve in our new house, I was sitting on my bed remembering the carols we'd sung in church, the candles we held when we sang— missing the beauty of it—and I started to cry. My father heard me crying, came into my room, and asked me why I was upset. When I told him he said, "Get dressed! We're going to church." The love of my father—a man who not only understood my love of the church, but also saw and honored who I was—was a huge gift to me.

I went to college to, essentially, become an ecologist, but ecology was not yet part of our vocabulary let alone a recognized science, so I studied related sciences and worked at the University of Colorado's Arctic and Alpine Institute collecting environmental data. The silence and beauty of the Rockies at 14,000 feet was a spiritual experience. The purity of it was something I wanted more of. I didn't think of my connection to Nature as a spiritual thing; I literally felt I was communing with the living planet. It never occurred to me that religion could give me these same kinds of experiences. Once I began meditating, Nature became my *ishta,* my most cherished aspect of God.

Eventually, I decided not to get a doctorate and took additional courses in Museology and learned to design educational museum exhibits. After I graduated college, I got a job at the American Museum of Natural History and moved to New York City. By the time that job ended four years later, I was a full-fledged hippie. I had no idea what to do next so I took a trip to California. While I was there I took acid and had a profound experience of Truth.

When I returned to New York, I was confused and deeply depressed. I was now actively searching for Truth, but I didn't know where to look for it. One afternoon I slammed my fist on the table and said, "Jesus Christ, if you exist, prove it to me!" The next instant, I felt a surge of tremendous joy and began dancing around my apartment exclaiming, "He exists! Jesus exists!" In *The Divine Romance*, Yogananda says we should "mean business with God," be earnest when we call to Him, and I couldn't have been more earnest! Or astonished! As a result, I became very interested in the spiritual life and began reading about various gurus and religious practices. I found a wonderful new job and my life slowly began to fall into place.

Two months later, I was invited to a dance concert on the other side of town. It was very cold that night and I wore a heavy woolen shawl from Guatemala to keep warm. I was waiting for the subway when a young Hispanic man approached me and asked about my shawl, curious to know if it was made in his village. We struck up a conversation. I mentioned the dance concert. It turned out he was a dancer in that troupe and would have been performing that night had he not hurt his back. We rode the subway together and he invited me to the cast party after the performance.

As it happened, my future husband was also a dancer in the troupe. He, too, went to the cast party. We had a brief conversation; I gave him my phone number, then left the party. He called every day that week. I knew it was him, but I was hesitant to answer the phone. I finally took his call on Thursday and agreed to go out with him Saturday night.

The moment he walked into my apartment, I felt I knew him—as if we'd known each other forever. He felt the same way. We could hardly talk; we just looked at each other. We eventually walked to his apartment and he made dinner. Afterwards we went for a walk and held hands. At some point during our walk, he turned to me and said, "I think we're going to spend the next fifty years together." I looked up at him and said, "I think you're right."

The following weekend we decided to get married, leave the City, and live on a commune. Six months later, we flew to Denver and stood beneath a tree in my parents' backyard and recited vows we wrote before a Baptist minister who was a friend of my family. Our wedding rings hung in little baskets from the branches of the tree we were married under. Our flute player gave us *Autobiography of a Yogi* as a wedding present.

I'd known about the *Autobiography* since college, but I could never gather the courage to go into a bookstore and say, "Do you have a book by Paramahansa Yogananda?" It was such a mysterious name. After the wedding, we tossed the book in the backseat of our Volvo with our other wedding gifts and set out to find a commune. We ran into an old friend of my husband's who offered to let us camp on some land he had in Northern California. We found the land, set up camp, and sat on a log by a lake and read the *Autobiography* together, page-by-page. Within a few minutes, we both began to weep, feeling that every question we had about our life, about Life, was being answered. When we finished reading the book, we embraced, knowing Master's teachings were now our life.

We threw away our grass, stopped eating meat, and became "yogis." We had no idea what to do next, no idea about the SRF Lessons, and no place to live, but we were committed. We drove down the Coast and met a man who invited us stay with his family for a while. We sat at his dinner table that night and listened, astonished, as he said Master's prayer for food. Then he told us about the Lessons.

Six weeks later we made our way to Washington state and stayed with friends for eighteen months. Now that we had a permanent address, we signed up for the Lessons. We read our first lesson on Thanksgiving Day. Though we didn't really understand what it was we were doing, we meditated every day, faithfully read the Lessons, and loved God together.

In the spring of '72, we settled in the Bay Area. One day, we heard about the SRF Meditation Group in Berkeley and went to Thursday night service. We knocked on the door of this house and a hippie with long hair and an army blanket draped over his shoulders invited us in. He'd turned his whole living room into a temple. Another devotee joined us and the four of us meditated. Afterwards, we sat on the floor and talked about SRF. This other fellow mentioned he lived in an elegant 19th century house with a double-door garage we could turn into a chapel, so that's what we did the next weekend.

From then on, we gave our lives to Master's work. We never questioned it. It was like coming home. We got Kriya from Brother Achalananda at Mother Center—the first Kriya he ever gave. Eventually sixty devotees came to the Center. In 1974, a group of old-timers—several of whom knew Master—acquired the Richmond Temple. Everybody helped renovate the building. Working together for Master deeply bonded our Temple community.

Master made many trips to Northern California during his lifetime, planting seeds for the future of his work in the Bay Area. Once we had the Temple, we held a class series with Brother Anandamoy, and our membership grew. I've been a service reader, Sunday school teacher, special events chair, and outreach chair—for fifty years. We recently acquired a beautiful new Temple in Walnut Creek and are on the threshold of a whole new era for Master's work in the Bay Area. My husband and I are as involved as ever.

I don't really have a favorite passage in the *Autobiography*. All of Master's writings are a source of guidance to me in the moment I read them. The teachings are like a telephone line to God. Every time I read the *Autobiography* I get something new from it. It hits you differently each time you open the book depending on what you need to understand at that moment, and goes deeper each time you read it. It becomes the living presence of God's love for you.

Shortly after we first read the *Autobiography*, I wrote the following letter to Sri Daya Mata:

> Dear Daya Ma,
>
> My husband and I just got married and were given the *Autobiography* as a wedding present. We read it together on our honeymoon and were overwhelmed

by Yogananda's teachings. Now we think
we should get a divorce and join the
ashram.

She wrote back—air mail, special delivery.

No, no my dears! In this life you are to
be householders!

So, we moved forward. Like all householders, like all married couples, we've had our share of challenges. We are two very different people. Anytime you put people together, it's like stones rubbing against each other. We know we're here to learn certain lessons. Knowing this makes us more compassionate and respectful. Meditation helps us be calm inside and listen to the other person. We've been banging up against each other for a long time now and we're getting pretty smooth.

Master's teachings and serving his work help us, as he says in *Scientific Healing Affirmations*, "chisel our lives to his design." We are devotees first and marriage partners second. Being loyal to his teachings helps us be better marriage partners and better friends. And perseverance furthers.

TWELVE

Hello, Playmate!

I am the husband referred to in the previous story.

I was born nearly eighty years ago in Buffalo, New York, the eldest of three sons. Our parents defended their Catholicism, but discouraged any expression of genuine spirituality, particularly my own early spiritual interests. As a child, I had an intimate relationship with Jesus and his Mother, and my devotion embarrassed my parents. On one occasion, my mother told me I looked "too holy" in church and that she and my father were concerned I would become a priest when I grew up. However, one day when I was about ten years old, I was helping paint the dining room and had the distinct thought, totally out of the blue, that I wouldn't "be in a monastery in this lifetime"—an interesting choice of words for a young boy to use about a religious vocation. From that time on, I knew I wouldn't be a priest when I grew up.

Our family was poor. Although my father was extremely smart, he dropped out of high school to support his mother, brothers and sisters, and took a low-paying job in the post office for the rest of his life. He was a very unhappy and angry man and took his unhappiness out on his sons. My mother was a homemaker and worked part-time in a bank. She lived in my father's shadow, almost as if she were invisible. She didn't know how to handle her creative and unconventional sons, so she routinely ignored us.

When you're a child, your whole world is your parents. Mother and Father love is intended by God to help prepare us for life, but I knew the way my parents treated my brothers and me wasn't right, and that I couldn't count on the adults I should have been able to count on. As a result, I distrusted authority and it became difficult for me to trust God. Master's teachings helped me learn to pray to the Heavenly FatherMother. I don't say "Father and Mother," I say "FatherMother," as one word, and I picture God—Who is, as Master says, both maternal and paternal—as my divine parents. Though I didn't have the love of parents in this lifetime, I insist on it now from my Divine Parents.

I was a solitary, somewhat introverted child, but I was a good student. I did a lot of acting and public speaking in grammar school. In high school I had a public speaking teacher—Ms. O'Meara—who took an enthusiastic, almost motherly interest in me. With her support, I got a full scholarship to Yale and off I went. I give my thanks to her all the time.

The Yale course catalog was a candy store to this bookworm. I could have gone to school there for the rest of my life just taking classes! I initially studied politics and economics, but in the end, I wasn't interested enough in these issues to make a career out of them. In my sophomore year I was recruited for a secret Catholic Order, but that was not to be. I left the Church that year and never looked back.

My best friend in college was in Navy ROTC and went to sea. His experience helped me to realize I wanted to go to sea, too, so after I graduated college I went to Officer Candidate School and became a Navy officer for three years. I discovered after-the-fact that I was involved in the Cuban Missile Crisis, but it was so top secret I didn't know about it at the time it was happening!

When I got out of the Navy, I didn't know what to do with myself. I was interested in social work so I applied to Columbia, got a scholarship, and moved to New York City, but the program was not right for me and I dropped out of within the year. I began acting again in several well-known experimental theater companies in the City, and took a dance class that led to my getting involved in several modern dance productions.

I was not aware of any spiritual yearning in me at that point in my life. In fact, there was a fierce battle for my soul going on inside me and I often indulged in behavior that was self-destructive. Fortunately for me, Master had his eye on me. I remember walking by a bookstore every day on my way to dance class and noticing a book in the window that repeatedly caught my eye. One day I went into the bookstore and asked the clerk about the book. He said, "That's *Autobiography of a Yogi*, by Paramahansa Yogananda." I asked him how much the book cost. Whatever it was seemed too expensive for me at the time, and I was out the door! But there he was, every day, greeting me on my way to class.

One night, after a performance I was dancing in, I saw a woman walk backstage and thought, "Wow!" Later, at the cast party, we struck up a brief conversation and I got her phone number. There was no voicemail in those days, so I called her on Monday, on Tuesday, on Wednesday, and again on Thursday before she finally answered her phone. We made a date for that Saturday night.

What happened next was like something out of a movie: I cooked her dinner at my apartment—liver and onions and spinach. (What was I thinking? It must have been a spiritual test for her! Could she fall for a man who served her liver and spinach?) Then we walked through the fog down to the Battery overlooking the Statue of Liberty. During our walk, I had the strong feeling we were going to spend the next fifty years together, so I told her what I was feeling. She agreed. And we have.

Within six months, I stopped dancing, my future wife quit her job, we left New York City, flew cross-country to Denver, and got married in her parents' backyard. Someone gave us the *Autobiography* as a wedding present. On our honeymoon, we sat on a log by a lake in the Napa

Valley in Northern California and read the *Autobiography* together, page-by-page. It was as if we had both been struck by the same bolt of divine lightning. From that point on, Master's teachings were our life.

After a fruitless eighteen-month search for a friendly commune to call home, we found work in the Bay Area. With my wife's help, I continued my theater work, and a show we did in San Francisco drew six hundred people. So, we settled in, continued to meditate and practice the teachings on our own, and got Kriya in 1974.

It wasn't long after we arrived in the Bay Area that we made our first visit to the SRF Meditation Group in Berkeley for a Thursday night service. Four people came to the service, including us. The next weekend we began helping one of the devotees we met that night convert his garage into a chapel. More and more people started coming to the services, and this led to the creation of the Richmond Temple. By the time we acquired that property, I'd given up my coveralls, gotten a haircut, become a service reader, an usher, and started to use my theater experience to produce plays at the Temple for India Night. This continued for the next fifty years. It was as effortless as breathing. Now, we have a wonderful new temple in Walnut Creek, and my wife and I are, once again, doing whatever we can to help make a spiritual home for Master's devotees in Northern California.

Though we've been together a long time and we share Master's teachings, we have our challenges like any other married couple. When difficulties come we've learned to respect each other's opinion, and we always try to keep our sense of humor alive and well. Most importantly, over the years we learned to acknowledge each other as unique souls presenting themselves to the Universe. Like that theory in physics—that *how* we see things determines *what* we see and experience—we help each other manifest our soul nature by seeing the other as the soul. It's exciting!

As we get older, there are new challenges to deal with. Relatively soon, given our ages, we are going to be separated. There's not going to be another fifty years! We do not dwell on the future, and we're ready to go. In the meantime, we stay right here, right now, in the present moment, serving Master and each other.

My favorite thought from Master's teachings is the last line of the last verse of his poem in *Songs of the Soul*: "Hello, playmate! I am here." I want to be Master's playmate, to be like a child—have the innocence and purity, the openness and detachment of a happy child—the child I didn't get to be in this life.

I once heard a wonderful story about Brother Bhaktananda that illustrates this idea. Brother was very childlike. Sometimes, he gave services that were good, and sometimes he gave services that were not so good. Either way, he didn't care. What he did didn't affect him. He ended every service he gave with the same equanimity, the same joy, he began it with. That's what I'm trying to do with my life.

Soon after we got married, my wife and I hung a large photograph of Master taken at the Lake Shrine Dedication in our meditation chapel. He smiles at me each day with unconditional love—whether I have a good meditation or not. One day, his smile was so strong and deep I had to look away. I realized afterwards that I'd seen that smile on the faces of fathers when they see their newborn babies.

When my life is done, I will look at that picture of Master at the Lake Shrine and see his unfailing smile and know he's grinning at me, his playmate. Then, he and I will both burst into laughter.

THIRTEEN

Thou and I Never Part

I'm a Jungian analyst. I've spent my life working with the inner world. It's been the primary domain of my life. Even before I became an analyst, even as a child, what was happening inside me was of far greater interest to me than what was going on in the world.

I was born in Huntington Park, California, just south of L.A. I am, as of this day, ninety-two years old. I'm married. My wife left the body almost ten years ago, but we are still married in Spirit; our marriage did not end because she is no longer in form.

I had seven children, five biological children and two children born to my wife. I adopted them when we married, and they have been with me most of their lives.

I was the fifth of six children. We were a close family. My father was a high school teacher. He taught shop classes. My mother stayed home with the children. I was baptized in the Presbyterian Church and went to church every Sunday with my family. It was an important part of our life, but the Presbyterian idea that you did not experience real happiness until you died and went to heaven made no sense to me. It seemed far-fetched. If this were true, I thought, then what was life here on Earth all about?

Two events from my childhood shaped my life. When I was seven years old, my grandmother died. Though I'm certain she was only trying to help me feel better about my grandmother's death, my mother told me that if you are a good person here on Earth, you go to heaven forever when you die. I was only seven, already quite bored with the world, so the thought of going any place "forever" scared the hell out of me.

The second event happened four years later when I was eleven. I had a brother who was three years older than I am, whom I loved very much. He was an integral part of my life. He had been very sick all his life, then he got well, then he got a cold, then pneumonia, then he died quite unexpectedly. His death was an enormous loss for me.

He was a special boy. He had visions and lived in two worlds—in this one here with us and in the astral world with friends. I'd always had the feeling there was more going on here on Earth than met the eye, and my brother's visions—just being in his presence—proved to me that what I believed about life on Earth was true. Losing him took away that context, and I completely fell apart. I repressed all my desires to know more about that unseen reality and lived on the surface of things. I somehow managed to get through school, but those years were oblivion to me.

By the time I got to college I was an agnostic and an atheist. I thought spirituality was "silly stuff." I took a couple of classes in religion that were interesting, but they didn't settle anything for me. They just raised more questions in my mind. The whole reason I got a doctorate in psychology was so I could understand what this world was all about. When I did my oral exam before my doctoral committee— some of the finest psychologists I ever knew—I realized they didn't have a clue about the purpose of life any more than I did! And if *they* didn't know what this world was all about, what would happen to me? With that thought, a cold wave of fear went through me.

My spiritual life began to emerge after I got my Ph.D. and began my own Jungian analysis. I spent a good ten years deeply examining my inner life and I got a lot of things worked out, but something was still missing. I didn't know what that was, but I knew I had to find it.

When I started doing therapy with others, I—out of necessity—dug even deeper into myself, into my own thoughts and feelings. I began to understand that the answers to my questions about life were inside me, not out there in the world. This was an enormous realization that changed my life! It allowed me to acknowledge and value my own thoughts and experiences, and to see, as Master says in the *Autobiography*, "… a divine universal plan exists and it is beautiful and full of joy."

Soon after I had this realization I heard an interview the BBC did with Carl Jung. At one point during the broadcast, the interviewer said, "Well, now, Dr. Jung, do you believe in God?" Jung kind of sputtered, then he stuttered, then he hesitated. Finally he said, "I don't *believe* in God, I *know* God!" That did it for me! I didn't know Jung personally, but I knew enough about him to know he had used his powerful mind to understand what God is. He knew God, and he *knew* he knew God! Listening to him, I suddenly understood it was God I was looking for! I began to read Vivekananda. I worked with my dreams. My inner life became very real and I could see meaning in events that I'd never seen before. It was tremendous!

My professional life was booming by then. I had a very successful practice, but my marriage of fifteen years was in shambles and coming to an end. Sometimes, no matter how hard you try, things don't work out. This was the case for me. It was very painful.

I was drawing and painting a lot then to try and sort out my feelings, and I decided to take an art class to help me figure out what to do about my marriage. On the first day of class, I walked into the art studio and noticed a woman painting quietly in the back of the room. I didn't know who she was. I looked over to where she was working and she looked up at me. Our eyes locked for a moment and I thought, Oh dear! This is *big* trouble! There was no question in my mind she had to be an intimate part of my life. I knew it—just like that. I was so stunned

I couldn't catch my breath. It was terrible and beautiful at the same time!

Over the next few months I got to know her a little bit. One day she gave me a copy of *Autobiography of a Yogi* and said, "You might want to read this." She'd been on the path ten years by then; Master was her life. I read the book—actually, I read half of it and stopped reading, not because I didn't need to read more, but because I was so full of Master's truth I couldn't take any more in! I eventually finished the book some months later and over the years, I've read it many times.

I started reading the SRF Lessons and began to meditate a little bit. I got the techniques and started practicing them. I'd been aware of Spirit and God before, and I had long wanted to live in a spiritual way, but you can't do what you don't know how to do! Now—as a result of doing Master's techniques—doors opened inside me! I could calm myself to the point where I was able to think about God and actually perceive Spirit, and I began to pay attention to who I was as a soul. Everything I did—even the ordinary things I'd always done—had so much meaning to me. This wasn't a permanent state of consciousness, but rather something I moved in and out of. I knew Spirit was there, but It was not always available to me, and I missed It when It was gone. This was amazing to me, almost unbelievable. It wasn't that I felt I didn't deserve God, but more that I hadn't *done* anything I could understand to experience God. It was as if God slipped in when I wasn't watching!

One day, maybe about a year into my practice, I went for a walk in the woods by myself and realized that all my doubts about the meaning of life, all my wondering whether I'd ever know the purpose of it all, had vanished! What life on Earth was all about, why I was here—to find God—finally was clear to me! Master was my guru! He would guide me! I was no longer alone! I was stunned! I still didn't like everything I had to do here, but I understood everything had a purpose—even the things I had to experience in my life I didn't like.

Within the year, I was divorced. I hated to go through it, but it was clear there was no other choice. About a year later, in 1967, I married the dear woman who brought me to Master in San Francisco. We took Kriya together from Brother Anandamoy in the afternoon, and after the service, he set up a little table before the Kriya altar and married us.

We were together fifty-five years. She continues to play a big role in my life though, as I said, she is no longer in the body. Three or four years after she died someone asked me if I was going to get remarried. I was shocked by the question because it never occurred to me I wasn't still married. She was, is, and will forever be my wife.

She was not a perfect mate, nor was I, but she always took me to God. She was very intuitive and knew things long before I did, long before they happened. She had an awareness—and gifts—I didn't have, a conscious perception of the angels Master says are waiting for us to give them the opportunity to help us on our journey. She taught me there is more to life than I can see or know in the present moment. One day she said, "I know why you love me. It's because I have my hand in God's." It was the truth. Living with her made the path real for me.

My spiritual life began when I read the *Autobiography* and it is still, after all these years, a go-to book for me. When I start reading it now, it's hard to stop. So many answers! So much inspiration! It's like it's alive. Sometimes, I'll read a sentence or two and think I could spend my whole life on just those few words. I have an original copy of the *Autobiography* that Master signed. I hold it and think, "Master held this in his hands!" It's thrilling.

Master is and always has been the central focus of my life, but when I experience Master, when I read the *Autobiography*, something of my wife is always there. She brought me to him not just that day in the art studio, but throughout our marriage, even in her death. Master in her is what I love most about her.

FOURTEEN

Always in His Grace

I'm a thirty-nine year old mother of three wonderful children, a full time mom and yoga teacher, currently living in Austin, Texas. I was born and raised in Encinitas, the youngest of two children. My father came to America from Chennai, India for graduate school in up-state New York. After he graduated, he returned home to marry my mother. Theirs was an arranged marriage in accordance with Indian custom. They had a short, small wedding by Indian standards—a three-day ceremony for a thousand people. They recently celebrated their 50th wedding anniversary.

After the wedding my parents returned to America, to Boston, where my dad started work. A year later they moved to San Diego. Master welcomed them to the path on the day they hand-delivered a letter to Sri Daya Mata as a favor for a relative who was a member of Guruji's society in India. Once they knew Paramahansa Yogananda was their guru, they moved to Encinitas to live close to the Temple and serve his work. Master found them the right house and they opened our doors to the devotees.

Our home was more than just the place where we lived; it was a sanctuary where we shared the essence of Master's Motherland with others. We celebrated our Indian selves with *bhajans* every Friday night and *pujas* on auspicious days. We'd chant for two hours and perform *arti*—an offering to God of *prasad*—then enjoy a potluck supper of homemade Indian dishes. This went on for twenty-five years.

My parent's core values were meditation and service. This was how they lived their life. They cleaned the Temple, cooked India Night meals, hosted Indian visitors, were ushers, assisted the monastics—they did it all. I did what they did from the time I was a small child because what they did looked good to me. I saw how important it was to nourish people not only physically but emotionally and spiritually, and I *wanted* to serve. Being part of something so helpful to others made my participation more meaningful. I helped prepare for the *bhajans:* I set the table, dusted, and placed the flowers on our altar. I enjoyed, most of all, welcoming people into our home, especially those who didn't have the anchor of family.

I also participated in the *bhajans.* My parents never forced me to meditate; they never said, "You better do what we do;" they said, "This is what we do." I never felt compelled to meditate because they did, or pressured to follow a guru because they did. I *wanted* to meditate. I knew when I was five this was how I'd live my life.

We were blessed to have a comfortable life, but my parents did not chase after material things. When my dad came home from work, he'd meditate before dinner and before he played with us kids, and my mom woke early every morning to do her *sadhana* before we got up. Meditation was their priority, and they consciously balanced their *sadhana* with raising their children. We knew we were a priority, but we also knew God was *the* priority. Their actions taught me that when I put God first, and put my whole heart into whatever else I did, I wouldn't have to worry about the rest of it. My dad's favorite saying—something I now say to my own children—is, "You do your 25 per cent and the rest is the grace of God and Guru."

Their service and devotion to Master enriched our traditional Indian life. We also existed within the American culture. My father was a nuclear engineer and was passionate about his field; my mother was a registered nurse and had many talents. I had the best of both worlds.

I also learned about service from my brother. He is ten-and-a-half years older than I am and is quadriplegic—the result of an accident at birth. I grew up assisting him with his daily activities—helped him with his meals, pushed him in his wheelchair, and so on—yet ours has always been a typical brother/sister relationship. He teases me and likes to joke around, sometimes at my expense! Some people can't get past his physical disability. They don't realize there's a normalcy there within our family, it's just not their normal.

The opportunity to hang out with someone who's different is a blessing, especially because he never complains or has a sour attitude. He prays for others before he worries about himself. Being around him as a child reminded me we are bigger than our bodies, that we are so much more than what we appear to be.

My grandmother came to live with us right before I was born. She was a very spiritual woman. She saw the trueness of the guru reflected in my parents' practice and adopted Master as her guru. She participated in SRF events, often wrapping saris on India Night, and enjoyed the fellowship of other devotees. Our large SRF family helped ease the culture shock of her move from India to America.

People who find Master on their own always have a story about how they found him. I don't have that story. I didn't have to find Master; he was always a fact of my existence, an agreement I made with him long before this incarnation. SRF was my path, and my gurus were my gurus. If I had a bad dream or felt scared, I'd think of Lahiri Mahasaya and Swami Sri Yukteswar and know whatever was swirling around me would be taken care of. I knew they heard my thoughts, and I heard their guidance. When I felt devotion to Jesus or Babaji or Hanuman or Ganesha I understood this, too, was part of my path. There was always room at my table for more!

Education is very important to Indian families. Because God is a part of everything my parents do, I went to a private Christian school through the twelfth grade.

Though I got a good education, it was difficult to be in an environment where everything about me was not their norm. My classmates would tell me I wasn't going to heaven because I didn't believe what they believed. I knew the bigger view—that the Christ Consciousness was bigger than what was here on earth, with or without the Christ body—and I realized how lucky I was to have Guruji help me understand this. I wanted to fit in, but I knew theirs was not my group mentality, that I wouldn't be able to participate in their world. I also knew I was on the path that worked for me. I remember consciously choosing to follow Guruji when I was in kindergarten. This, then, is *my* story: I did not have to find Master, I only had to put my trust in his grace.

To make sure I understood the differences between what I heard in school and Master's teachings, my mom arranged for me to regularly talk with Sister Shanti. Sister taught me Christ's message—that all we can really do is love the person who is hateful to us. She also helped me understand that we are all evolving in different ways, that all souls and all religions do not approach life in the same way. She taught me that we each come to earth to experience what we need to experience, so we see things based on our life experiences and what each of us has to learn.

There were still things that were difficult—the racism was hard. There were times when I felt anxious about our differences. So Sister taught me about the ways the Bible and Master's teachings were the same. She also taught me a seven-year-old's version of the "Peace and Harmony Prayer," and breathing exercises I could do when I felt upset or hurt. I learned to fill my body with light, then step into that light and wrap it around me. And she helped me remember that each of us has a soul and an ego, and not to take what an ego says to me as important. When someone was cruel, I'd think, "This fight's not for me. I don't need to get involved in their issues," then let them shadow box themselves. I was meditating every day at home and that really helped.

I also had teachers who saw the person in me, and that made a big difference. I loved learning and that's what I wanted from this school. I also loved to play sports. Most of my friends were boys because all they cared about was that I was a good athlete.

I hung out with my SRF friends on Sundays, and occasionally at the beach in the summer, but I didn't see them much beyond that. Girl's Summer Youth Program was a vital connection for me to other girls who loved Guruji and the teachings as much as I did and wanted the deeper conversation about God I longed for with my peers. It was the place where I got a concentrated dose of spiritual fellowship and made special connections with my peers. I'm still close to many of those girls today, and our kids play together when I'm in town.

I thought about taking Kriya as a teenager, but realized I just wasn't mature enough to put my whole heart into it and fulfill my promise to the guru. So I kept on meditating and serving, thinking I'd take Kriya when I was twenty-one. As my birthday grew closer, I got busy with finals and didn't send in my application. When I realized what happened, I meditated and said, "I'm sorry, Guru, but I'll take Kriya when I finish school."

The next morning, a nun I served with at the Mother Center during convocation called to say she'd been thinking about me. I told her I'd been planning to take Kriya but had missed the deadline. She said, "You need to take Kriya. It came to me in meditation." I knew Guruji was telling me it was time to do this, so she did my preliminary phone interview and I mailed in my application. I took Kriya at convocation. All the special people in my life attended the ceremony.

I first read the *Autobiography* when I was eight. My mom gave me a dictionary and a copy of the *Autobiography* for summer reading. Because I was such a good rule-follower, I was shocked and concerned to discover Guruji had disobeyed his elders and run away from home as a boy! (This was another conversation with Sister Shanti!) What I loved most were the stories of Guruji meditating in his attic room in Kolkata as a boy because I'd been there with my family and meditated in that room. I had a physical connection to the room—the sacred presence—that I call upon to this day.

The story of the silver amulet Guruji's mother left to him on her deathbed—that it would be there for as long as he needed it—is a touchstone for me about what Divine Mother and Guruji do for me, for us all. Things and people come and go for as long as that interaction is necessary.

There's a reason for every interaction but, of themselves, these interactions are not what's most important. They aren't what life is all about, nor are they necessarily good or bad. They're what we need to move us forward on the path of realization. We need a variety of experiences to give Guruji the opportunity to show himself in many shapes and forms and feelings. This is how he prepares our souls. This is what Omnipresence and Unconditional Love is all about.

"In sending loving thought vibrations to the thousands of Kriya Yogis scattered like shining jewels over the earth, I often think gratefully:

'Lord, Thou hast given this monk a large family.'"

—Paramahansa Yogananda
Autobiography of a Yogi

Epilogue

I'm a professional writer. Though my body of work includes many books, stories, interviews, and articles—
each one my favorite—*Coming Home* has been the most
surprising thing I've ever written. SRF devotees have been
telling me the stories about how they came to the Master
for four decades, so it was not as if the subject matter was
new to me or that I hadn't thought about writing a book
like this before—several times, in fact. Then one day, one
minute—quite unexpectedly—writing this book was nearly
all I could think about. The time had come for me to stop
thinking about it and actually do it. This was the first of
many surprises in store for me.

I began gathering my thoughts in August of 2019.
The Centennial Anniversary of Paramahansaji's coming
to the West was a mere thirteen months away. Collecting
these stories on the eve of such a historic occasion felt to me
to be a fitting tribute to the Master. Given the time frame,

pulling it all together would no doubt keep me hopping. I laid myself at the feet of the Divine Compassion, committed heart and soul to the project, and "hencedforth." I had no idea Covid-19 was also around the corner, that social distancing and sheltering in place would not only provide me with the time and space to get the job done, but also make the need for transcendent stories like these a requisite of daily life.

Given the number and beauty of the stories I'd heard over the years, I asked the Master to make it clear to me—to choose—who I would interview for the book. My experience as a writer also brought certain professional parameters to bear: to accurately, faithfully represent Paramahansaji's teachings, to include storytellers who span generations and represent various cultures and backgrounds, to remain true to each storyteller's voice, and to focus on the experience rather than the personality of the storyteller by maintaining the storyteller's anonymity. By design, I would present each story to the reader as I experienced it during the interview, as an intimate, memorable conversation.

What I did not foresee or even imagine when I cast my net was that I would be led to people who would also give voice to something the Master wanted to include in the book, that at some point in telling their own story Paramahansaji would lend his silent signature to their interview. There were moments in every interview—sacred turnings of the mind that gave these conversations wings—when the storyteller stepped out of the attachment we humans have to our own story and harvested their soul's capacity to embody some aspect of universal Truth. "Undreamed of possibilities" transpired, I believe, because of each storyteller's sincere willingness to offer up the most important story of their lives in service to something larger than themselves.

What moved me may well be different than what moves you. But the point of this little anecdote is that you know that just as the Master gathered the people to tell these stories, he now gathers the people to read them. Such is his omniscience and love.

What happens in these pages is not meant to stay in these pages. These stories *want* to be talked about with friends on the path, with friends who are searching for a path, with friends who have not yet expressed a desire for an intimate relationship with God. These stories help us recognize Divine Love in myriad forms, and prompt us to tend the most creative relationship of our lives: the ever-expanding kinship with the God of our heart that makes any life extraordinary.

We don't have to be perfect to set foot on this path. In fact, as these stories show, it's very common to miss the mark several times before we understand the import of a spiritual life. These stories prove that, when we are ready, a moment comes when worlds align and doors open that allow us a peek at Who we really are—at something so beautiful and natural and sheltered and intimate that it really does feel like coming home. This does not mean all our troubles go away, but that we know we are, as Yogananda says, "ever safe in the fortress of Thy loving care."

Our part is to become better stewards of our own consciousness, to be more aware of the effects of our thoughts and actions and choices, and be more emotionally generous with ourselves and others; to love God with all our heart, soul, mind, and strength and love our neighbors as ourselves. In the process, we become less attached to our likes and dislikes and our habits and limitations, and more attuned to the Divine Will. We see "signs and wonders" everywhere. We mythologize rather than pathologize. In so doing, our wounds become sacred and we become the stories that allow us to bear witness to others' lives.

From wonder unto wonder, existence opens.

God's Boatman

I want to ply my boat, many times,
Across the gulf-after-death,
And return to earth's shores
From my home in heaven.

I want to load my boat
With those waiting, thirsty ones
Who are left behind,
And carry them by the opal pool
Of iridescent joy
Where my Father distributes
His all-desire-quenching liquid peace.

Oh, I will come again and again!
Crossing a million crags of suffering,
With bleeding feet, I will come—
If need be, a trillion times—
So long as I know
One stray brother is left behind.

I want Thee, O God,

That I may give Thee to all.

I want salvation,

That I may give it to all.

Free me, then, O God,

From the bondage of the body,

That I may show others

How they can free themselves.

I want Thine everlasting bliss

Only that I may share it with others;

That I may show all my brothers

The way to happiness

Forever and forever, in Thee.

—Paramahansa Yogananda
Songs of the Soul

Acknowledgements

How do I begin to thank the extraordinary people who loved this book into the world—some I'd known for decades and others I didn't know until we met for our interview, then felt as if we'd known each other forever.

We came together in a variety of ways: me as "writer girl," they as advisers, champions, storytellers, and virtuosos in their respective fields, sisters and brothers—what Yoganandaji calls "friends once more to be." Everyone should have a posse like this, magic makers who believe in you and give of themselves in Paramahansa Yogananda's name.

Thanks be to the beautiful storytellers who offered up their hearts and stories on a silver platter; to Marianne and Muriel, my Book Mata's who nursed me along and continually raised me up; to Robert, Jerry, Silvia, and Chris, who supported the book's development; to Lucinda Lawton, who transcribed the audio interviews from Margaret-speak into English; to painter Donna Young at https://www.

donnayoung.com/ for her extraordinary painting "East End" for the book cover; to Teri Rider who designed the book and to Chelsea Robinson who proofread it—the mythic mother-daughter duo who love words and stories as much as I do; to my own mythic daughter Julie Faith who created my beautiful website and took the stellar photo of me for my website; to Lora Calcara for her windswept photo of me in this book; to John MacDonald, another mythmaker, who went over-the-moon with the video from the first moment I told him about it; to Gary Nicholson for his powerful song, "Choose Love," for the video soundtrack; to Wendy and Nancy who beta-babed the first draft; to Linda and Timmaris for their "can-do" support; to William who schlepped me to the airport in Minnesota in a car that smelled like muffins fresh from the oven in a menacing snow storm; and to the unnamed Delta pilot whose perpendicular jettison took the plane I was in high above that storm at warp speed and brought me safely home to sunny San Diego.

Thanks be to all of you who find something of yourselves in these stories and might one day say, "It was like coming home."

And to Paramahansa Yogananda—who makes everything I do possible and in whose arms this book now resides.

Permissions

My heartfelt gratitude to Self-Realization Fellowship for their permission to use Paramahansa Yogananda's image and words in this book from *Autobiography of a Yogi, God Talks With Arjuna: The Bhagavad Gita, Inner Peace, Songs of the Soul, and The Divine Romance.* All SRF books are published by Self-Realization Fellowship, 3880 San Rafael Avenue, Los Angeles, CA, 90065-3219, U.S.A.

"The Songs of Kabir," tr. by Rabindranath Tagore, XXVII, II. 81, p. 75, paperback edition 1977, Samuel Wiser, Inc. is part of the public domain.

Quotations by Carl Jung, Lao Tzu, and from the Bible are part of the public domain.

Glossary

Arti. An ancient Vedic ceremony inviting various aspects of God into one's heart. The ceremony includes traditional prayers and offerings to God of incense, flowers, candles, and specially prepared vegetarian delicacies.

Avatar. A Sanskrit word meaning a divine incarnation; one who has attained complete union with Spirit and guides others on their spiritual journey.

Bhajan. A traditional Indian song expressing devotion to God.

Commemoration service. A meditation service honoring the birth or passing of an SRF guru.

Convocation. An annual weeklong immersion in the "How-to-Live" teachings of Paramahansa Yogananda that includes classes in the SRF meditation techniques, group meditations, *satsangas*, *kirtans*, and pilgrimage tours. Held in Los Angeles, California and online, convocation is attended by SRF members from around the globe. Visit www.Yogananda.org for additional information.

Darshan. A Sanskrit word meaning the blessing of being in the presence of a saintly or deeply revered person.

Devotee. An ardent follower of a spiritual path or teacher.

Disciple - Direct disciple. A spiritual seeker who establishes a formal link with a guru and receives their training. SRF Lesson students become disciples when they take Kriya Yoga initiation. A direct disciple is someone who was personally trained by Paramahansa Yogananda during his lifetime.

Golden World Colony. Paramahansa Yogananda originally spoke of the SRF center in Encinitas, California, as the Golden World Colony. Built in 1935 on a bluff top overlooking the Pacific Ocean, the property includes a hermitage, a retreat center for SRF members, a monastic ashram for monks and nuns of the Self-Realization Fellowship Monastic Order, and public meditation gardens. The Golden Lotus Temple on the property slid into the ocean in 1942 when the cliff collapsed due to erosion.

Guru - Guruji. An enlightened spiritual master ordained by God to guide others to God. The Sanskrit syllable *gu* means "darkness," *ru* means "light." Thus, guru literally means one who takes the devotee from darkness to light. *Ji* is a Sanskrit suffix that denotes reverence and respect.

Gurus of Self-Realization Fellowship. The SRF lineage includes enlightened masters from the East and West: Paramahansa Yogananda, Jesus Christ, Bhagavan Krishna, Mahavatar Babaji, Lahiri Mahasaya, and Swami Sri Yukteswar.

Guru Gita. A Hindu scripture (*Song of the Guru*) chanted as a prayerful invocation to the guru.

Hermitage. The home built for Paramahansa Yogananda in Encinitas, California, by his disciple James J. Lynn, where the Master wrote *Autobiography of a Yogi* and other books.

Horn of Plenty Bank. A technique created by Paramahansa Yogananda for creating material and spiritual abundance that includes affirmation and right action.

Ishta. A Sanskrit word meaning "cherished divinity;" one's favorite form or aspect of God.

Kirtan. An Indian call and response form of group chanting that praises of God. Chants are accompanied by Indian musical instruments including the harmonium, mridanga (drums), kartals (shakers) and the sitar.

Kriya Yoga. The ancient and highest meditation technique taught by Self-Realization Fellowship. Kriya initiation is conferred only by appointed spiritual representatives of the SRF monastic order.

(The) Lessons. A home study course created by Paramahansa Yogananda that provides step-by-step instructions in the SRF yoga techniques of concentration, energization, and meditation, imparts practical guidance for every aspect of life, and presents techniques for learning to live joyfully and successfully in a changing world. For additional information, visit www. Yogananda.org.

(The) Master. One who has achieved self-mastery and union with God.

Mother Center. The international headquarters of Self-Realization Fellowship and Yogoda Satsanga Society of India in Los Angeles, California.

Paramanhansaji. A spiritual title that signifies spiritual mastery. The literal meaning is "supreme (*param*) swan (*hansa*)"—the swan being a symbol of spiritual discrimination.

Prasad. A Sanskrit word meaning the vegetarian food offered to God, often during a *puja* such as *arti,* then eaten by the devotee at the end of the ceremony.

Puja. A Sanskrit word meaning an act or ceremony of worship.

Sadhana. A Sanskrit word meaning the instruction and meditation practices followed by a disciple that lead to realization of God; a spiritual path.

Satsang. A Sanskrit word meaning a spiritual discourse.

Sharanam. A Sanskrit word meaning to surrender to or take refuge in the eternal love of God.

About the Author

I am, from birth, a storyteller. It's not just what I do. It's how I move through the world.

I have degrees in Art Therapy, Psychosynthesis, and Leadership studies. I lead retreats that tap the bounty of our collective wisdom and the power of creativity to reveal the truth and beauty of our inner lives.

Everything about the life I've lived is a good story. But *the* story, the heart and soul of my personal narrative, is that I am a disciple of Paramahansa Yogananda.

To learn more about my work, please visit:

www.ComingHomeStories.com
www.InSweetCompany.com

To learn more about Paramahansa Yogananda and Self-Realization Fellowship, please visit:

www.Yogananda.org